FOR ORGANS, PIANOS & ELECTRONIC KEYBOARDS

E-Z PLAY TODAY

54

Gospel Favorites

NEWLY REVISED

Hal Leonard Publishing Corporation
7777 West Bluemound Road P.O. Box 13819 Milwaukee, WI 53213

ISBN 0-7935-0537-2

Amazing Grace

Registration 2
Rhythm: Waltz

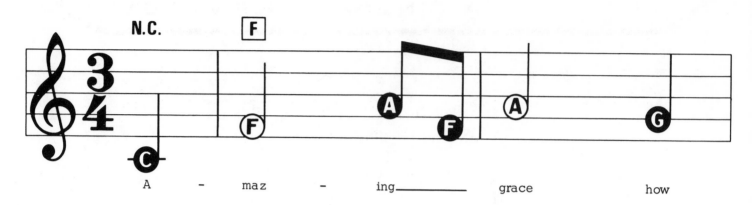

A - maz - ing_____ grace how

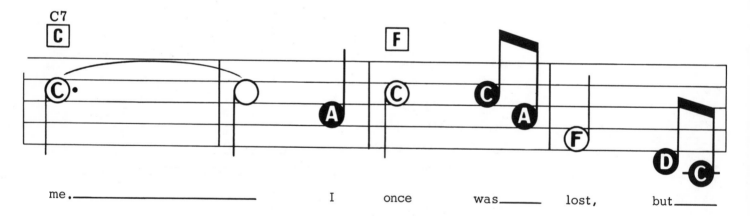

sweet the sound That saved a _____ wretch like_____

me._____ I once was_____ lost, but_____

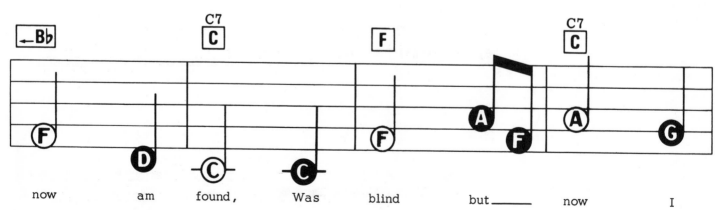

now am found, Was blind but_____ now I

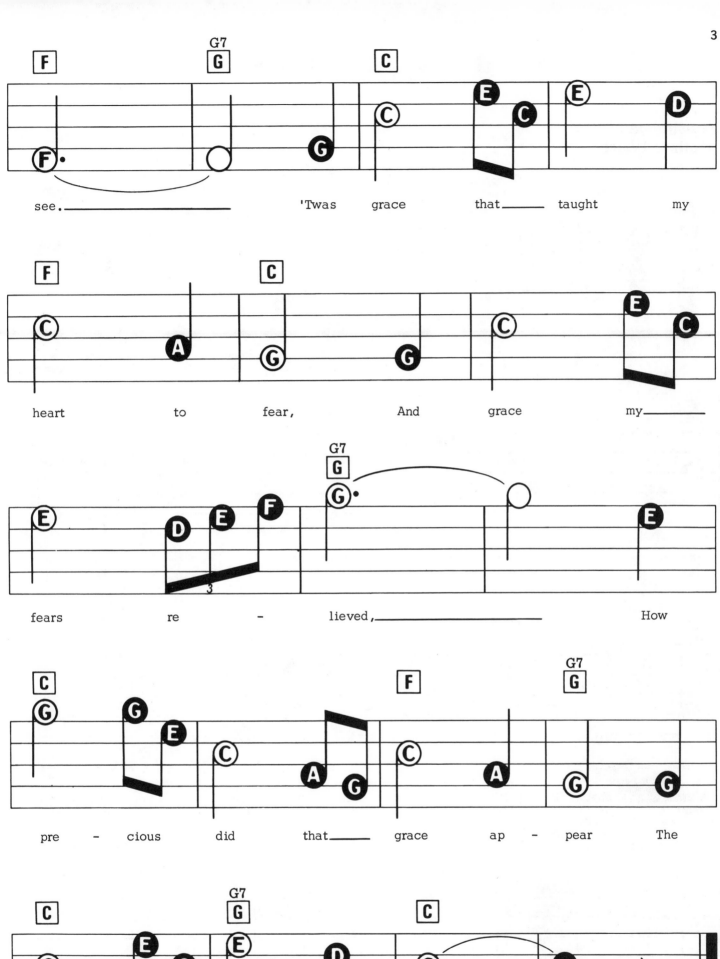
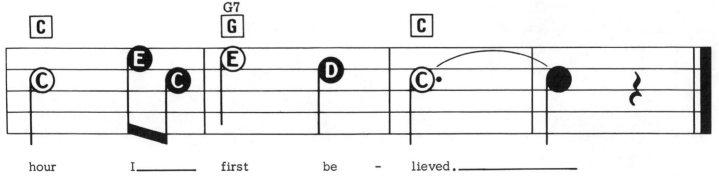

As We Sail To Heaven's Shore

Registration 3
Rhythm: Waltz

By Phill McHugh
and Greg Nelson

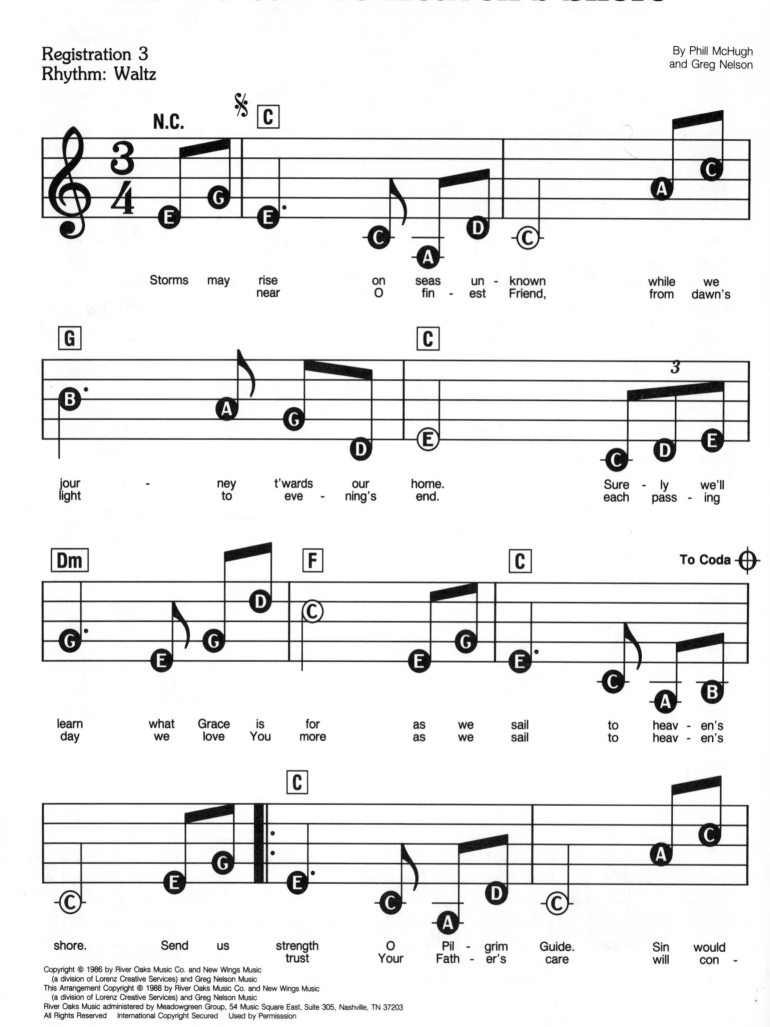

Storms may rise near on seas un - known while we
near O fin - est Friend, from dawn's

jour - ney t'wards our home. Sure - ly we'll
light to eve - ning's end. each pass - ing

learn what Grace is for as we sail to heav - en's
day we love You for more as we sail to heav - en's

shore. Send us strength O Pil - grim Guide. Sin would
trust Your Fath - er's care will would con -

5

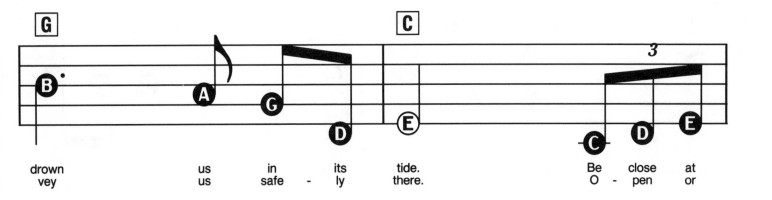

drown us in its tide. Be close at
vey us safe - ly there. O - pen or

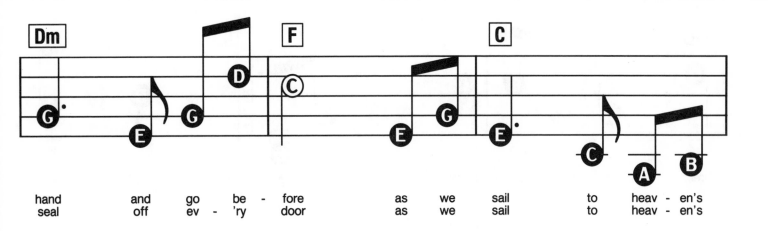

hand and go be - fore as we sail to heav - en's
seal off ev - 'ry door as we sail to heav - en's

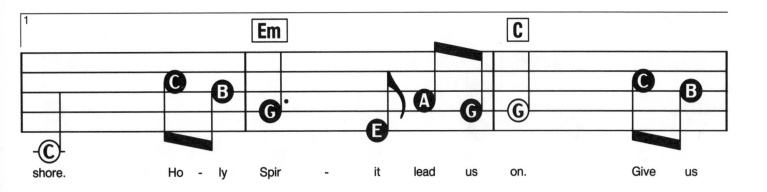

shore. Ho - ly Spir - it lead us on. Give us

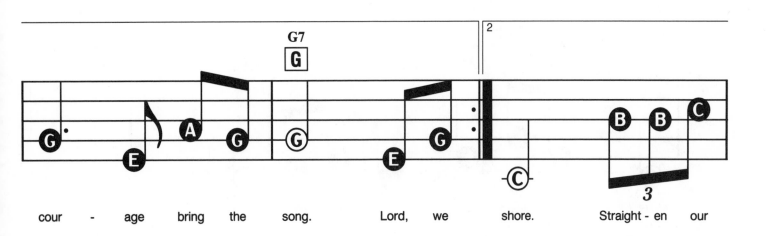

cour - age bring the song. Lord, we shore. Straight - en our

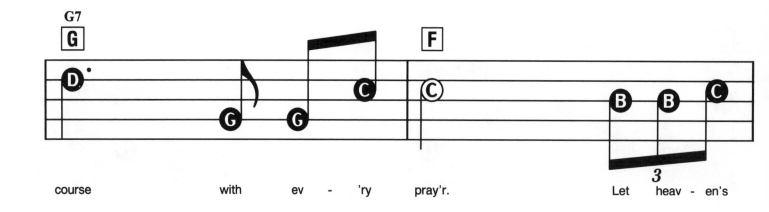

course   with   ev - 'ry   pray'r.   Let heav - en's

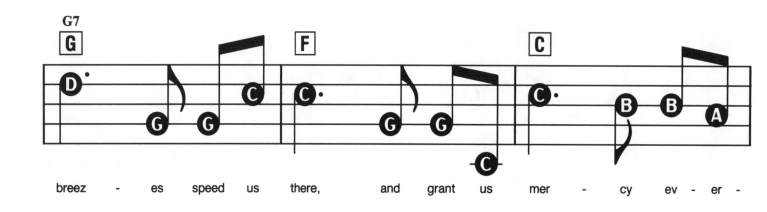

breez - es speed us   there,   and grant us   mer - cy   ev - er -

D.S. al Coda
(Return to %
Play to ⊕ and
skip to Coda)

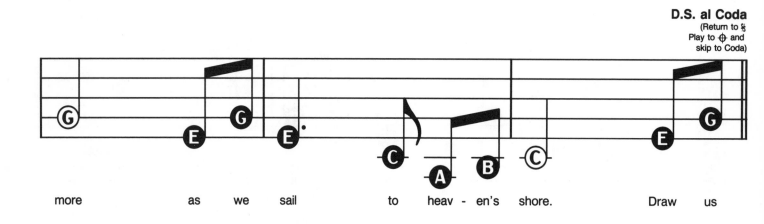

more   as   we   sail   to   heav - en's   shore.   Draw us

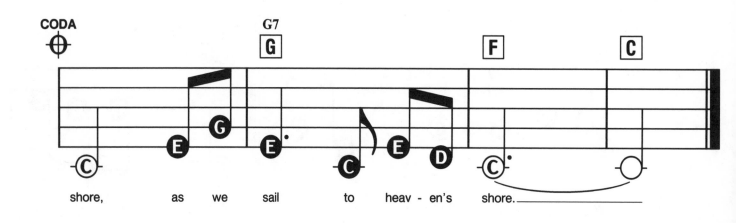

shore,   as   we   sail   to   heav - en's   shore._____

The Broken Vessel

Registration 2
Rhythm: Waltz

by Andrae Crouch

8

Send for a free catalog:

Name _____

Address _____

City _____ State _____ Zip _____

Age: ___ 12-20 ___ 21-30 ___ 31-40 ___ 41-50 ___ over 50

Music Preference: (check as many as apply):
___ Pop   ___ Standards   ___ Classical   ___ Country   ___ Heavy Metal
___ Folk   ___ Jazz   ___ Childrens   ___ New Age   ___ Rock
___ Other

Instrument: (check as many as apply):
___ Piano   ___ Organ   ___ Guitar   ___ Voice   ___ Portable Keyboard
___ Drum   ___ Bass Guitar ___ Other_____

CCB

HLP® Hal Leonard Publishing Corporation

7777 West Bluemound Road P.O. Box 13819 Milwaukee, WI 53213

PLACE
STAMP
HERE

Faith Of Our Fathers

Registration 10

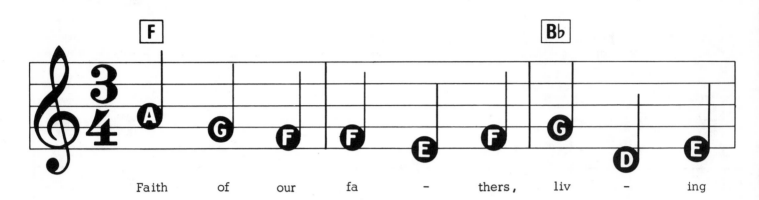

Faith of our fa - thers, liv - ing

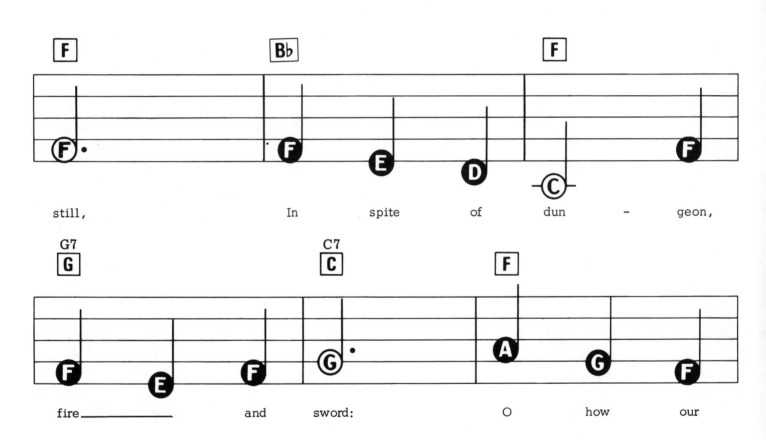

still,   In spite of dun - geon,

fire_____ and sword: O how our

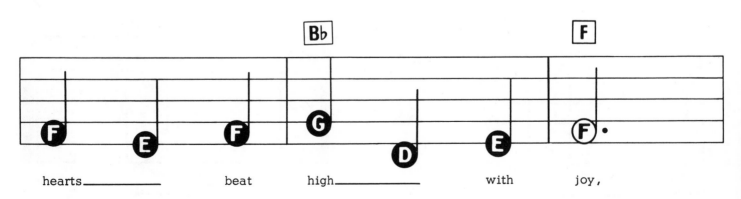

hearts_____ beat high_____ with joy,

11

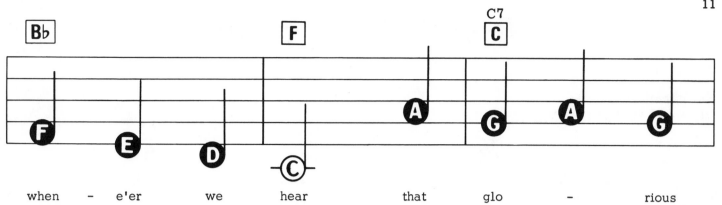

when – e'er we hear that glo – rious

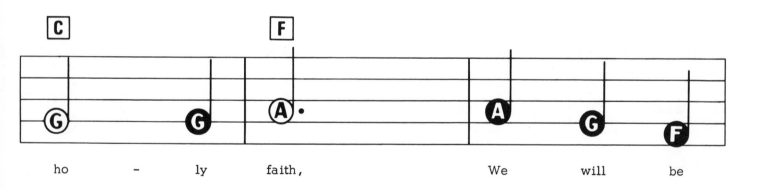

word! Faith of our fa – thers,

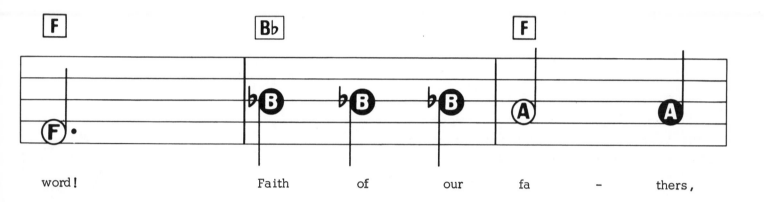

ho – ly faith, We will be

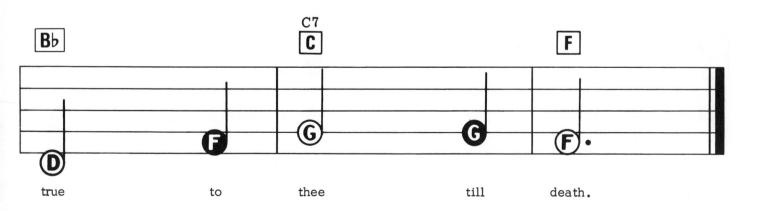

true to thee till death.

Gentle Shepherd

Registration 6
Rhythm: Ballad or Slow Rock

Words by Gloria Gaither
Music by William J. Gaither

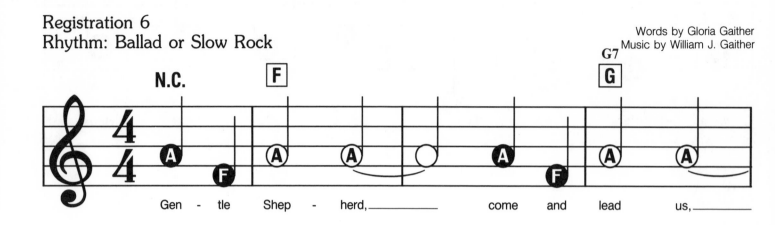

Gen - tle Shep - herd,_____ come and lead us,_____

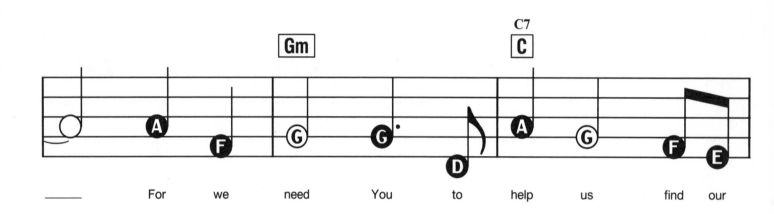

_____ For we need You to help us find our

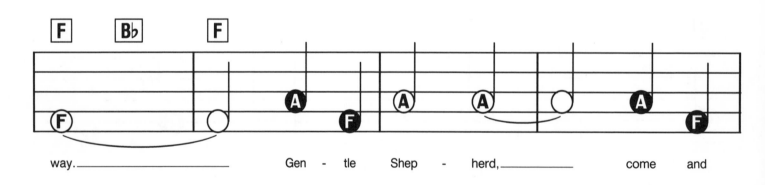

way._____ Gen - tle Shep - herd,_____ come and

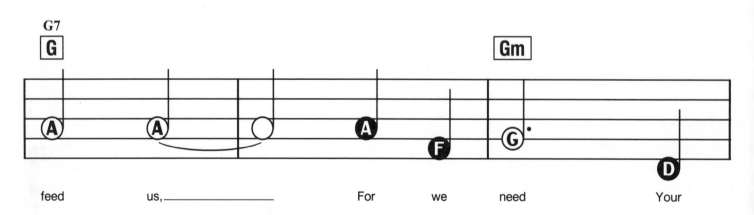

feed us,_____ For we need Your

13

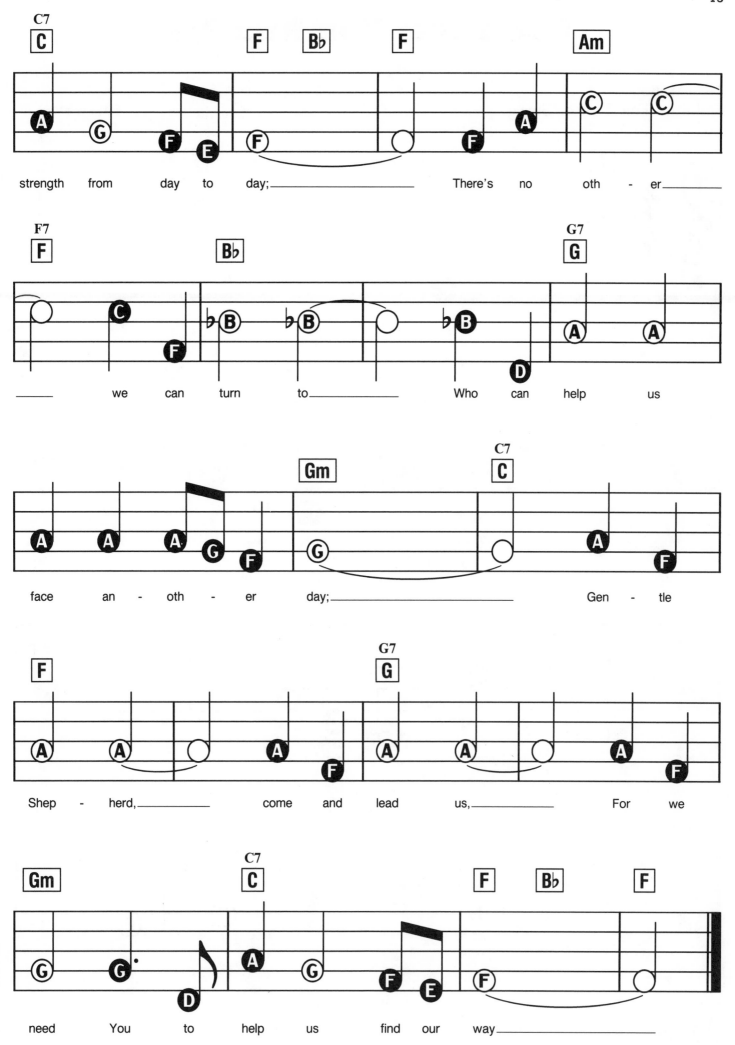

God Loves You And Me

Registration 5
Rhythm: Fox Trot or Swing

Words and Music by
Johnny Lange and Bill Norvas

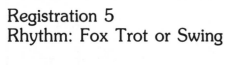

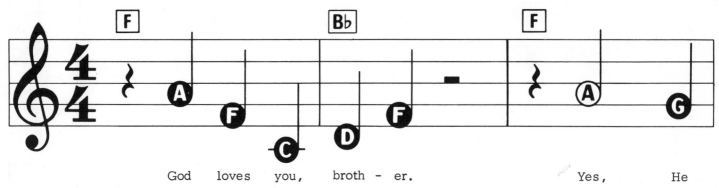

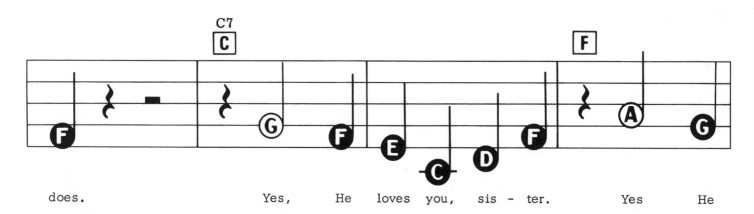

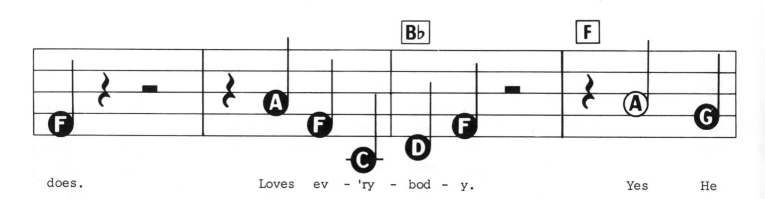

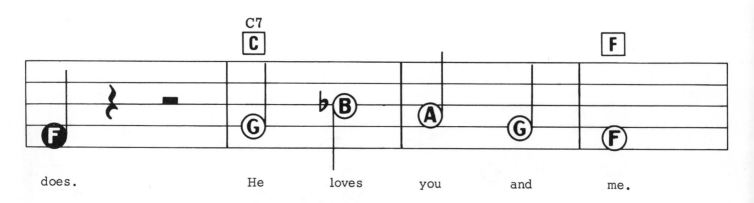

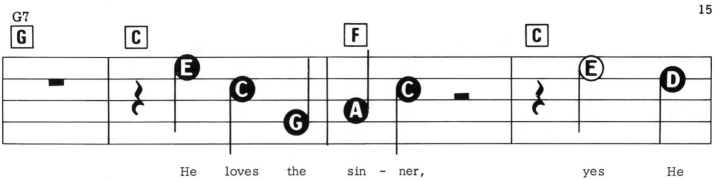

He loves the sin - ner, yes He

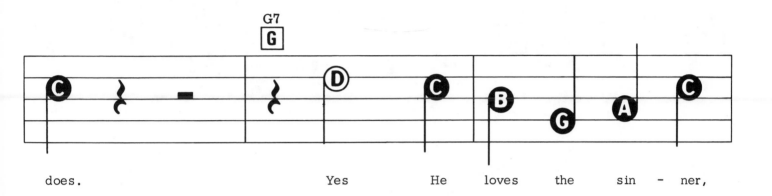

does. Yes He loves the sin - ner,

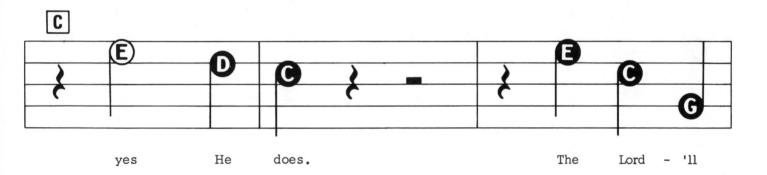

yes He does. The Lord - 'll

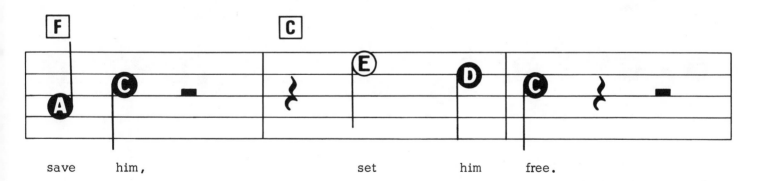

save him, set him free.

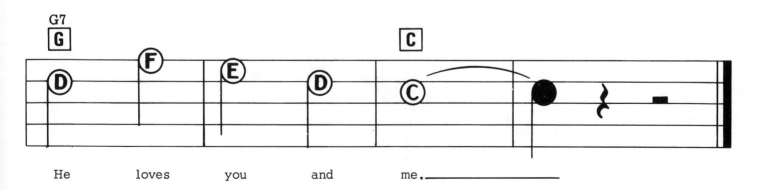

He loves you and me._____

Happy Is The Man

Registration 4
Rhythm: Rock or 8 Beat

Words by Herb Newman
Music by Herman Hammerman

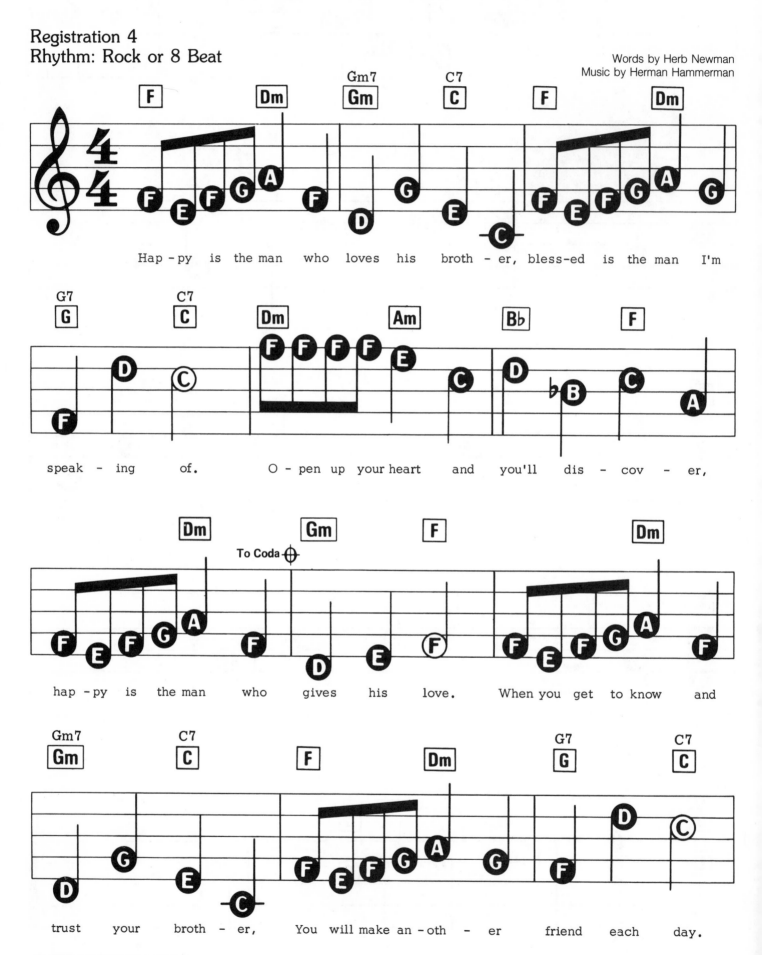

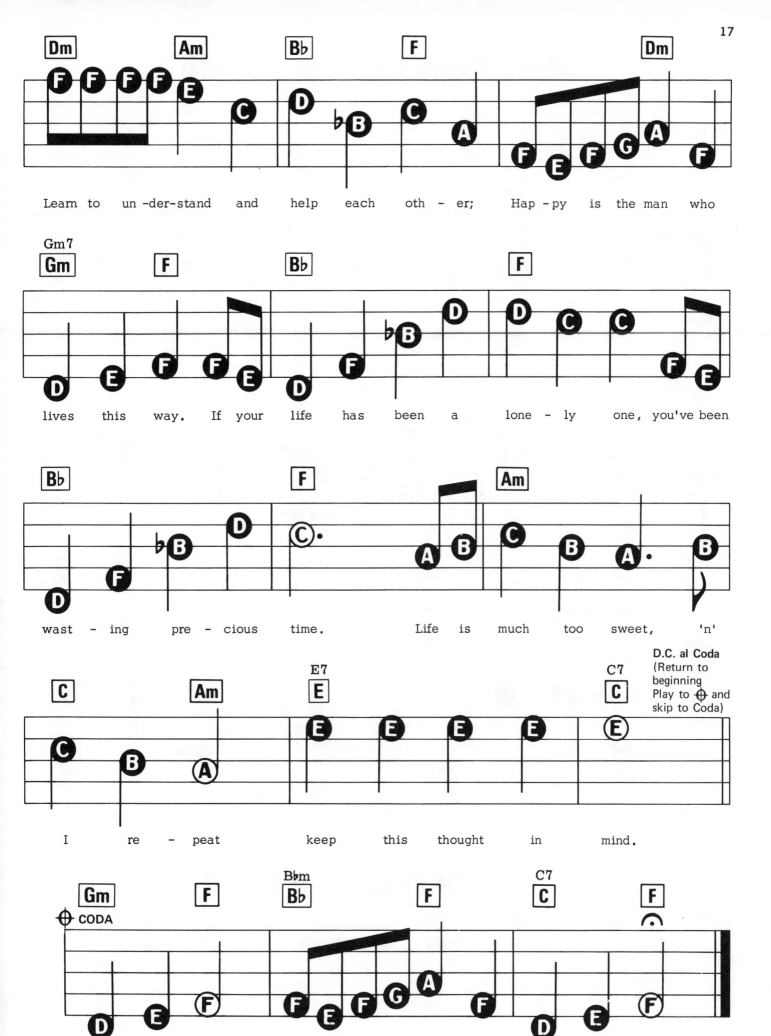

He's Everything To Me

Registration 9
Rhythm: Rock or 8 Beat

By Ralph Carmichael

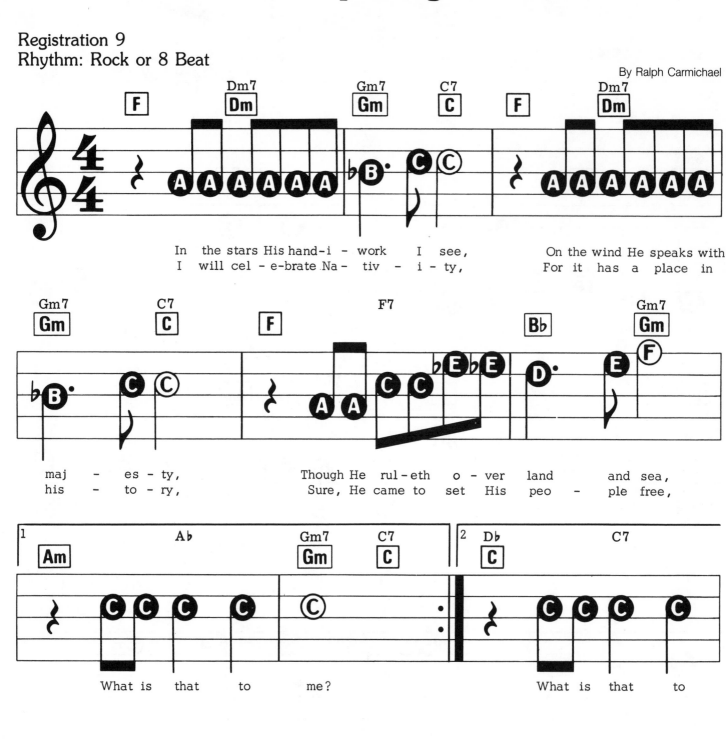

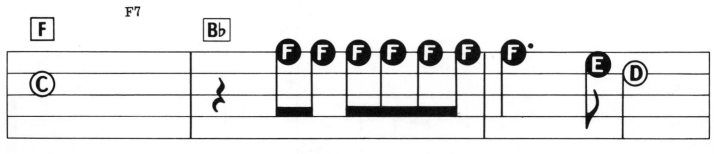

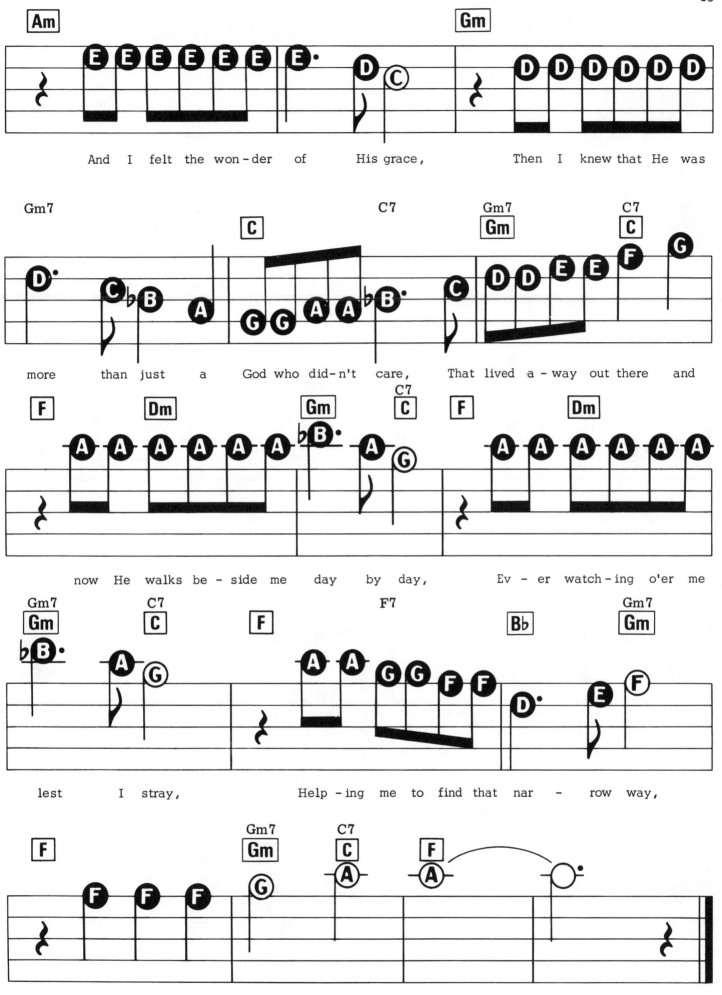

His Name Is Wonderful

Registration 3
Rhythm: Waltz

Words and Music by
Audrey Mieir

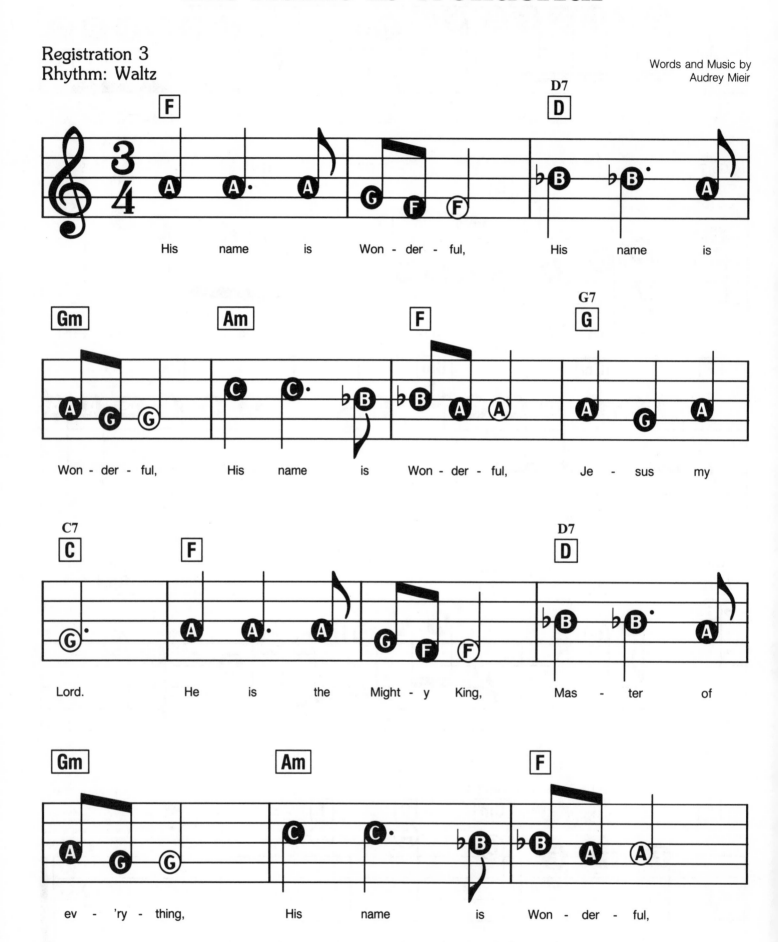

21

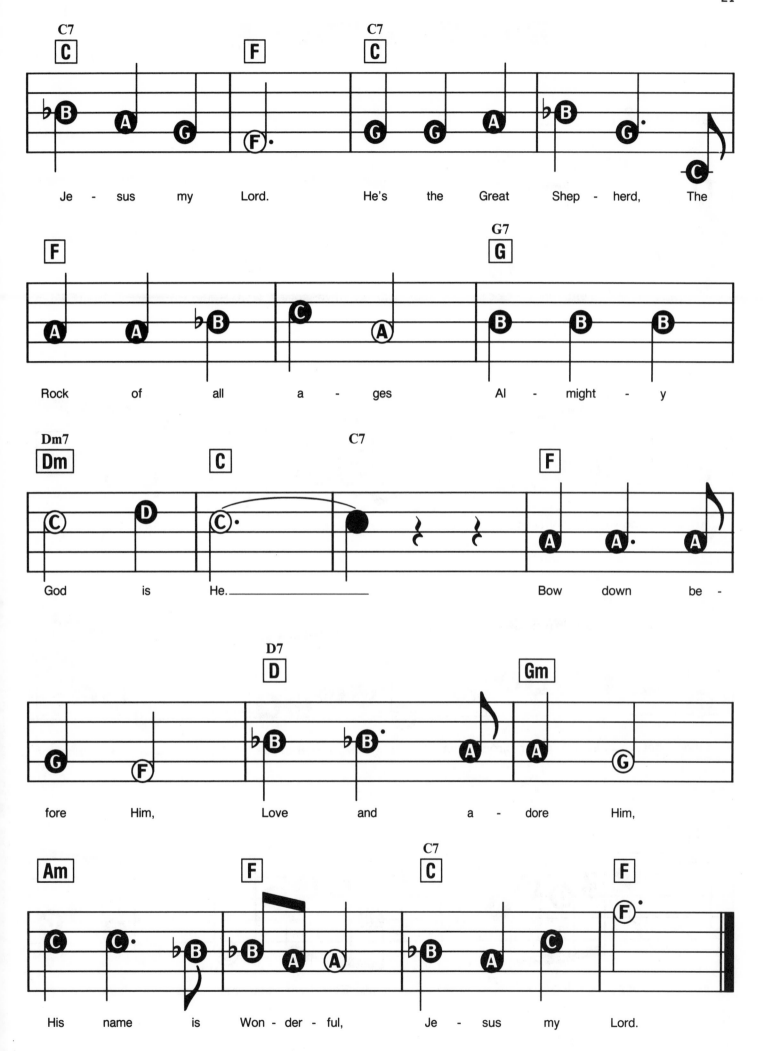

How Great Thou Art

Registration 2

By Stuart K. Hine

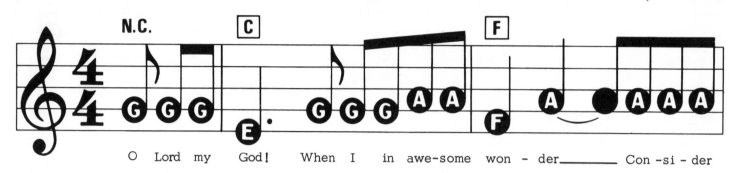

O Lord my God! When I in awe-some won - der_____ Con -si - der

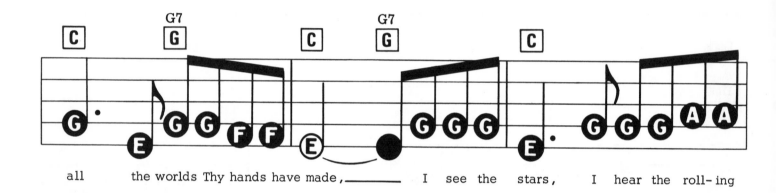

all the worlds Thy hands have made,_____ I see the stars, I hear the roll-ing

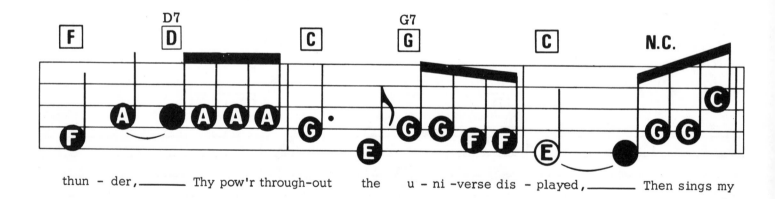

thun - der,_____ Thy pow'r through-out the u - ni -verse dis - played,_____ Then sings my

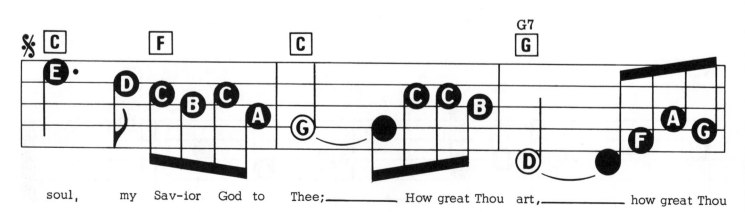

soul, my Sav-ior God to Thee;_____ How great Thou art,_____ how great Thou

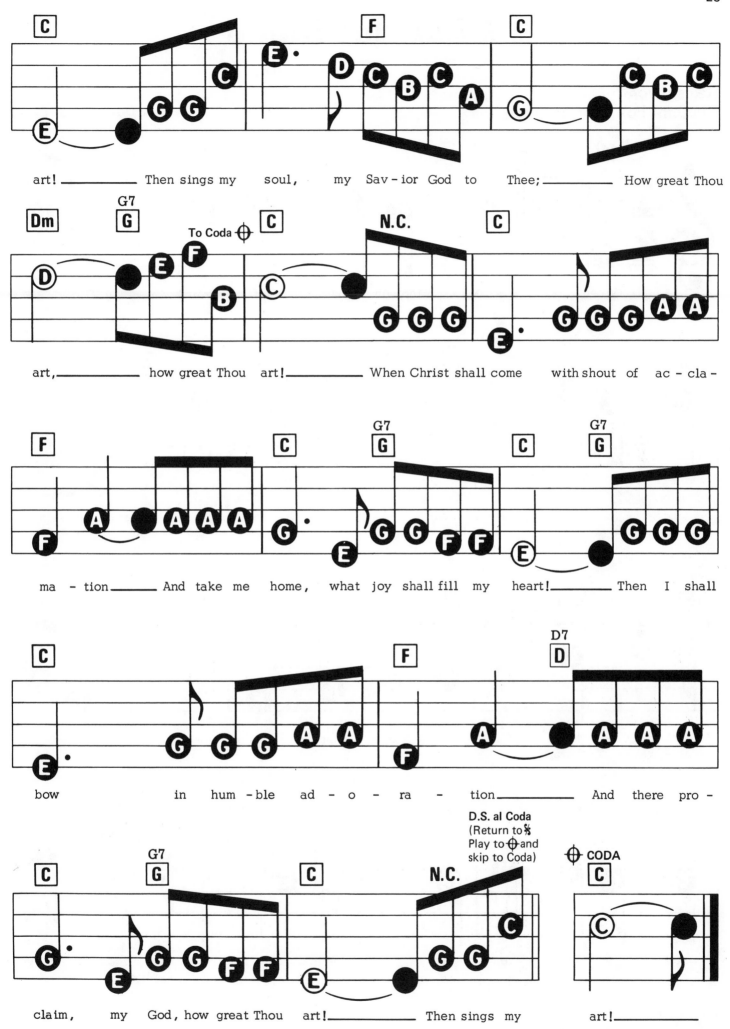

I Am Not Alone

Registration 5
Rhythm: Fox Trot or Swing

Words and Music by Johnny Lange,
Evelyn Merrill and Eddie Ballantine

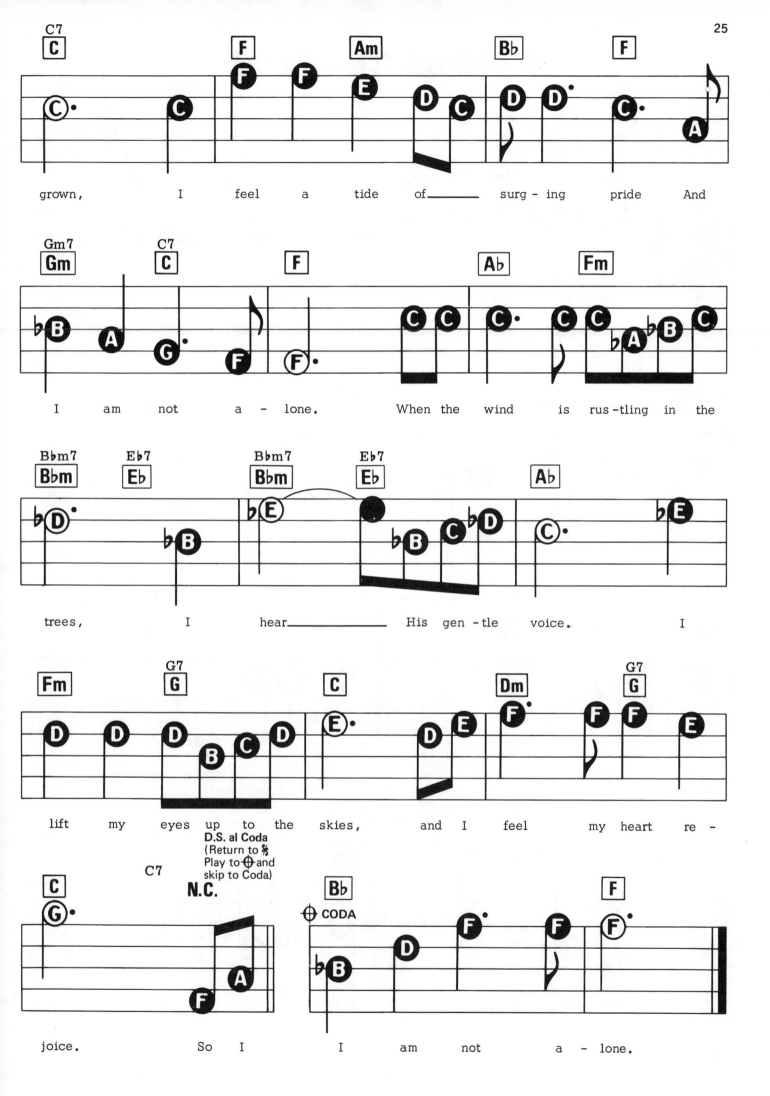

I Asked The Lord

Registration 4
Rhythm: Fox Trot or Swing

By Johnny Lange
and Jimmy Duncan

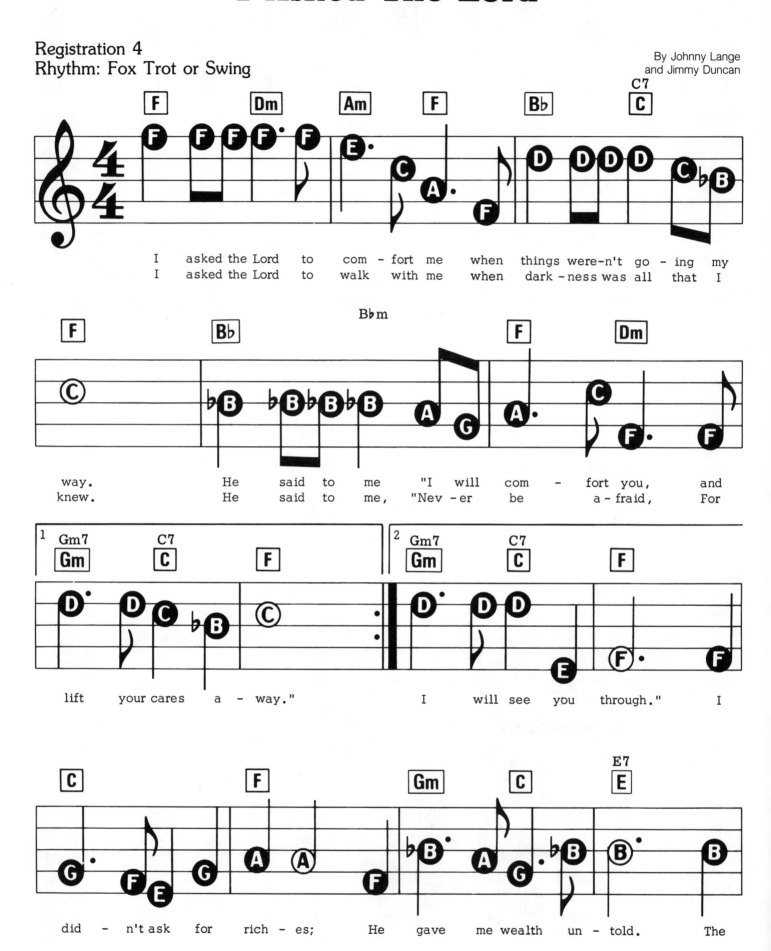

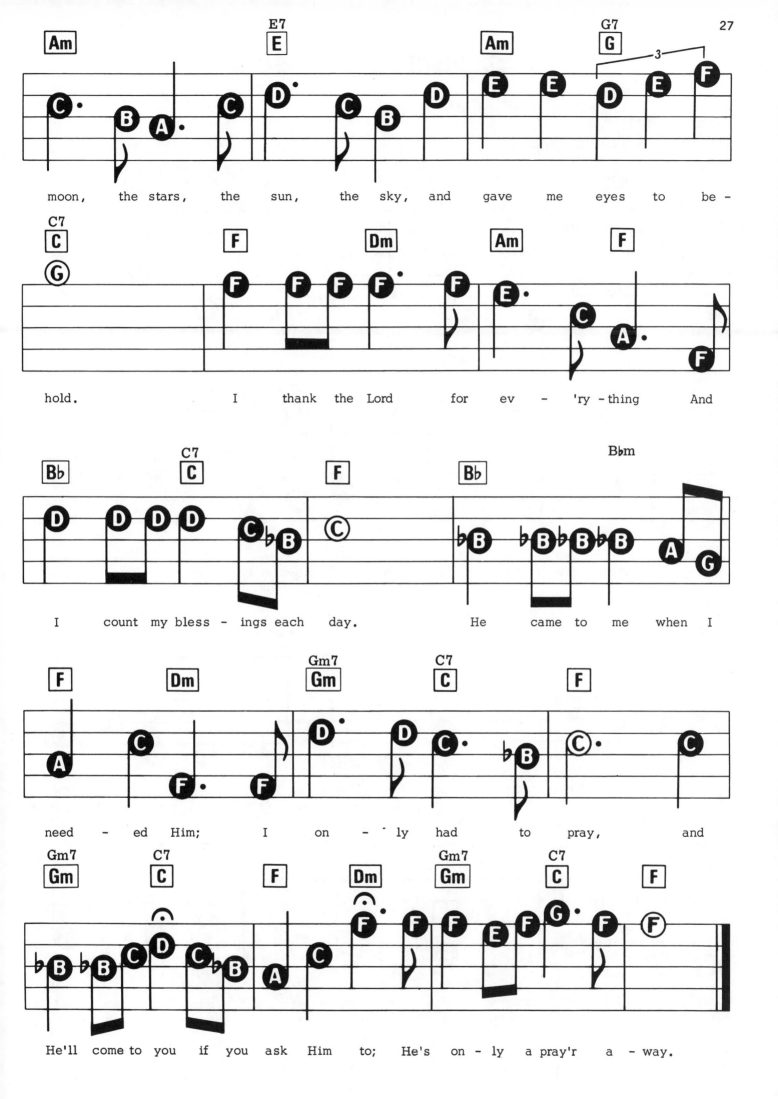

I Expect A Miracle

Registration 9
Rhythm: Fox Trot or Swing

By Ralph Carmichael

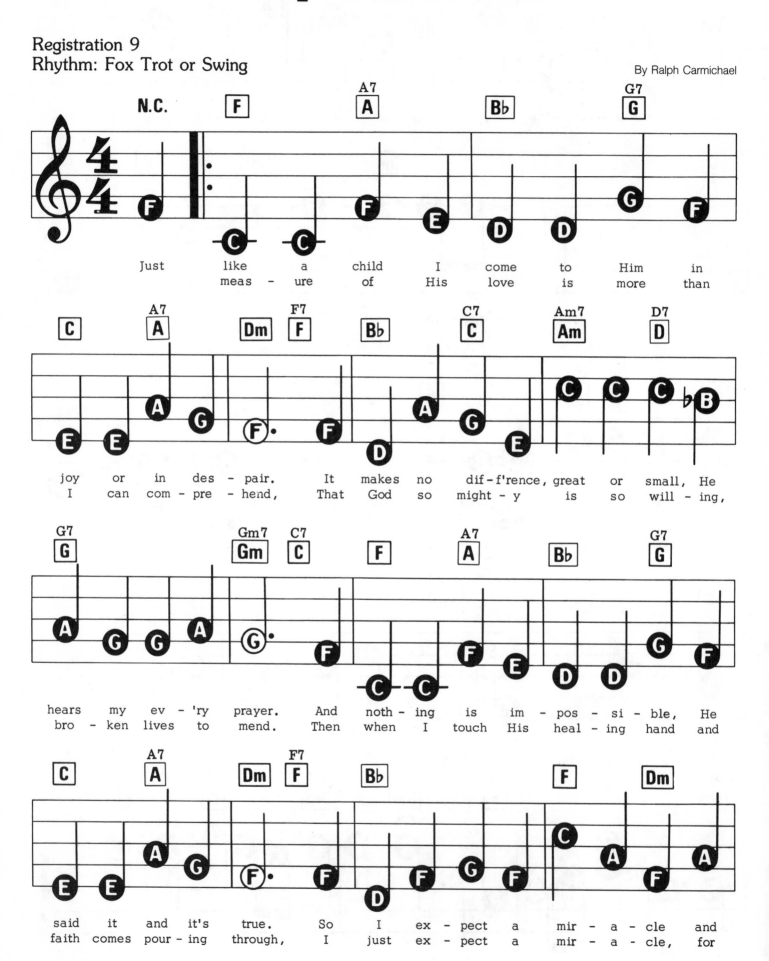

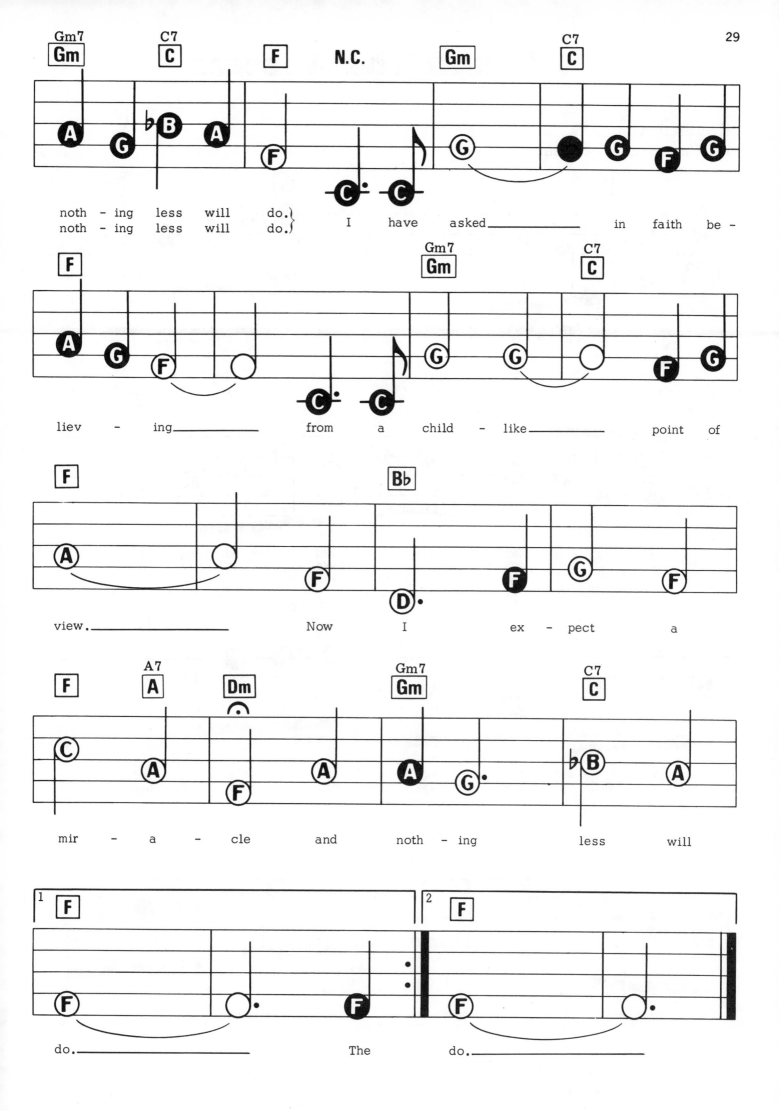

I Found The Answer

Registration 5
Rhythm: Rock or 8 Beat

By Johnny Lange

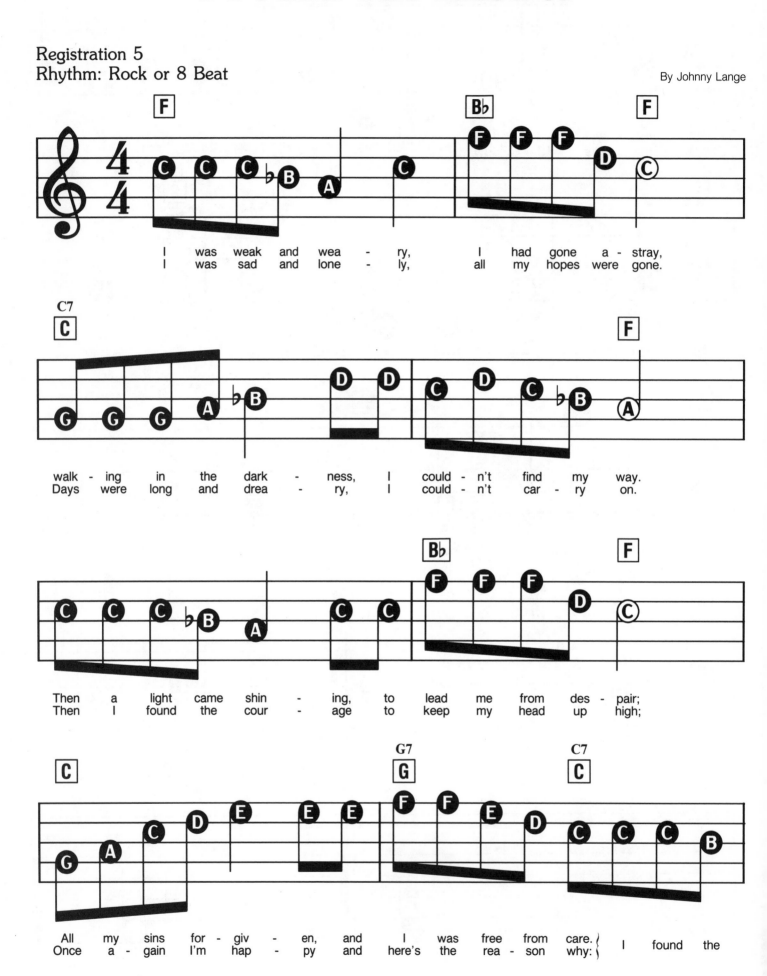

I was weak and wea - ry, I had gone a - stray,
I was sad and lone - ly, all my hopes were gone.

walk - ing in the dark - ness, I could - n't find my way.
Days were long and drea - ry, I could - n't car - ry on.

Then a light came shin - ing, to lead me from des - pair;
Then I found the cour - age to keep my head up high;

All my sins for - giv - en, and I was free from care.
Once a - gain I'm hap - py and here's the rea - son why: { I found the

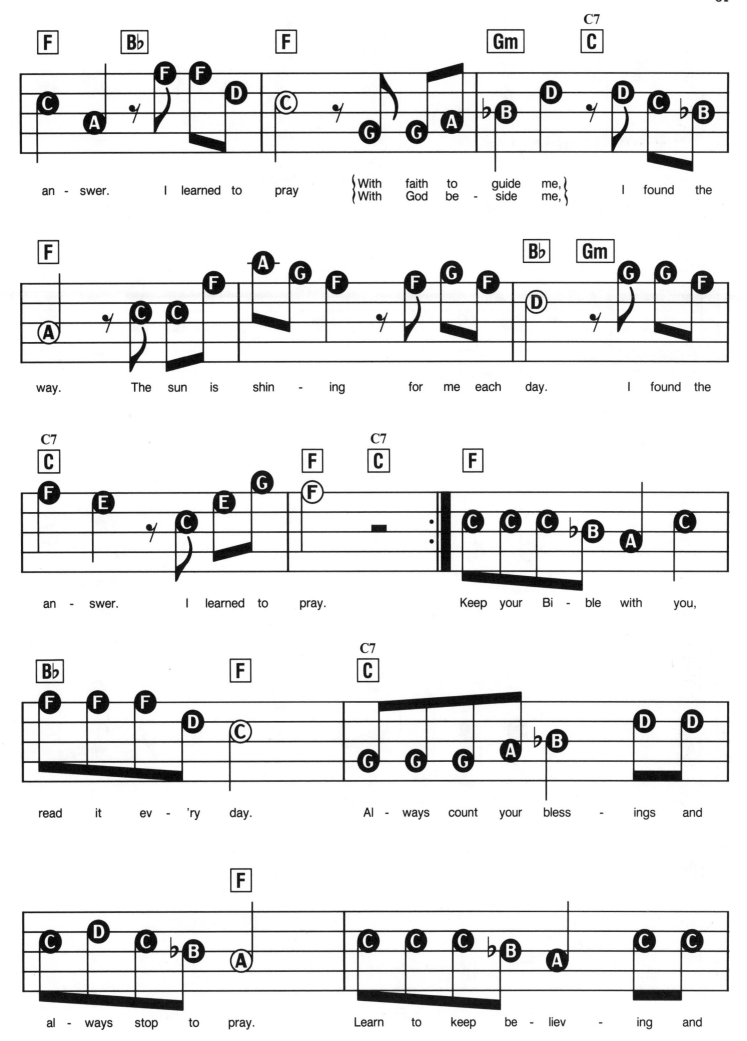

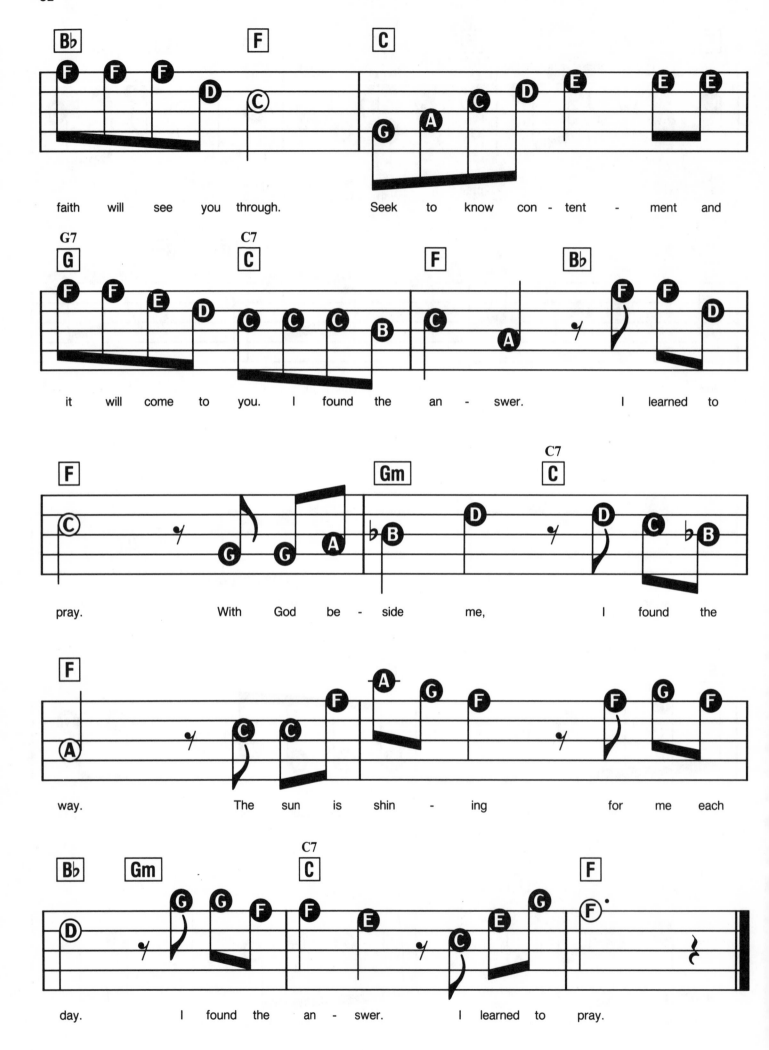

FOR ORGANS, PIANOS & ELECTRONIC KEYBOARDS

E-Z PLAY TODAY chord notation is designed for playing standard chord positions or single key chords on all major brand organs and portable keyboards.

BEGINNINGS—BOOK A $5.95   00100320
FUNDAMENTOS MUSICALES (SPANISH TEXT) $5.95   00100423
An introduction to the E-Z Play TODAY Music Series, including: When The Saints Go Marching In • Kumbaya • Beautiful Brown Eyes • Londonderry Air • I Gave My Love A Cherry. Also includes Keyboard Guides and Pedal Labels.

BEGINNINGS—BOOK B $5.95   00100319
Continues the instruction from BOOK A to provide the player with more advanced technique. Also features 12 more great tunes.

BEGINNINGS—BOOK C $5.95   00100318
Explains how to embellish E-Z Play Today arrangements. 12 songs: All Through The Night • Amazing Grace • Andantino • Dark Eyes • Fascination • Give My Regards To Broadway • Havah Nagilah • Joshua Fit De Battle Of Jericho • LaPaloma • My Bonnie Lies Over The Ocean • Silver Threads Among The Gold • The Whistler And His Dog.

BEGINNINGS SUPPLEMENTARY SONGBOOK $5.95   00101496
This supplementary songbook works with instruction books A, B and C in BEGINNINGS FOR KEYBOARDS. Each song in this book has a cross-reference to the song it coordinates with in the appropriate instruction book. 28 super songs, including: I've Just Seen A Face • Edelweiss • Stand By Me • Hello Again • Crazy • Earth Angel • Song Sung Blue • And I Love Her • It's A Small World.

BEGINNINGS COMPOSITE $19.95   00100317
A comprehensive instruction course that includes BEGINNINGS A, B, C, and Supplementary Songbook.

EXPLORING SERIES

E1. EXPLORING AUTOMATIC RHYTHM $5.95   00102102
A special edition teaching new techniques and various features of automatic rhythms on the electronic keyboard. Includes 12 songs, featuring: America • Can't Help Falling In Love • Neutron Dance • What Child Is This? • more.

E2. EXPLORING CHORDS $5.95   00102103
This edition teaches "fingered" chords. Includes 252 chord diagrams; explains what fingered chords are and how they are played ; presents charts of the most common fingered chords for every note of the scale and in every position. Also includes 8 great songs: Bewitched • Everytime You Go Away • I Left My Heart In San Francisco • In The Mood.

E3. EXPLORING PLAYING TECHNIQUES $5.95   00102104
This book lets the electronic keyboard player in on "tricks" to further enhance his/her playing techniques. For example, it teaches the player how to add variety and interest to any song by changing registration, adding grace notes, etc. 13 songs, including: Amazing Grace • And I Love Her • The Rainbow Connection • more.

E4. EXPLORING INTROS AND ENDINGS $5.95   00102105
This book reveals some of the secrets of the pros in creating introductions and endings for arrangements played on electronic keyboards. You can use these secrets to dress up and showcase your arrangements. "Exploring Intros & Endings" cuts through most of the technical material and gets to the heart of the matter, allowing you to apply the techniques learned right away. 11 songs included: Another Somebody Done Somebody Wrong Song • Can't Help Falling In Love • Climb Ev'ry Mountain • Crazy • Endless Love • People • more.

E5. EXPLORING DOUBLE NOTES $5.95   00102106
This supplementary book gives the keyboard player instruction on double notes, including the correct notes to play and how to come up with your own double note harmonies. It features 14 great tunes: Don't Cry For Me Argentina • Kumbaya • Somewhere Out There • The Entertainer • more.

E6. EXPLORING RIGHT HAND CHORDS $5.95   00102107
This book cuts through most of the technical material and gets right to the heart of how to add full chords to the melodies you play. A few basic principles are taught that allow anyone to sound good immediately. Includes 14 songs: A Bicycle Built For Two • Could I Have This Dance • Fascination • The Longest Time • Sweet Caroline • more.

E7. EXPLORING BACKING TRAX $5.95   00102112
Experience the fun of overdubbing with your keyboard's sequencer! This book teaches how to read Backing Tracks in an arrangement, how to record Backing Tracks into a sequencer, and how to use Backing Tracks as duets to play live. 9 songs including: I Write The Songs • Somewhere Out There.

Prices and availability may vary outside the U.S.A. Book prices, contents and availability subject to change.

KID'S KEYBOARD COURSE

BOOK 1 $5.95   00102133
This book teaches children how to use an electronic keyboard through easy instruction, color-coded notation and stickers, lots of illustrations, games and puzzles, and plenty of songs that kids will be able to play right away.

BOOK 2 $5.95   00102134
This book picks up the instruction where Book 1 ends and gets students into more aspects of making music. Like Book 1, it also contains lots of songs, puzzles, illustrations and fun!

DUET/BACKING TRAX

The arrangements in this series include both the melody and a second part to popular collections of songs. You can play both parts together with another player or by recording the melody or rhythm onto your keyboard's sequencer and playing along with it. Great tunes make these books fun to play!

D1. CHILDREN'S SONGS $5.95   00102084
17 songs to enjoy, including: Camptown Races • Humpty Dumpty • Hush Little Baby • Oh! Susanna • Old Grey Mare • On Top Of Old Smokey • Peter, Peter Pumpkin Eater • This Old Man • more.

D2. CHRISTMAS CAROLS $5.95   00102085
16 holiday favorites, including: Away In A Manger • Go Tell It On The Mountain • Hark The Herald Angels Sing • Jingle Bells • Joy To The World • Silent Night • We Wish You A Merry Christmas • What Child Is This?

D3. HYMN DUETS $5.95   00102086
18 beautiful hymns, including: Amazing Grace • Crown Him With Many Crowns • Holy, Holy, Holy • Just As I Am • Onward, Christian Soldiers • We Gather Together • much more.

D4. POP DUETS $5.95   00102087
8 songs, including: Can't We Try • Don't Know Much • Endless Love • Islands In The Stream • Somewhere Out There • You Don't Bring Me Flowers.

PLAY ALONG TRAX

Have you always wanted to play along with a professional band? With these great new book/cassette packs you can! These books come with a full band accompaniment cassette so you can play right along with the band and sound like a pro.

T1. CHILDREN'S SONGS $12.95   00102088
25 favorites to play along with, including: B-I-N-G-O • Camptown Races • Humpty Dumpty • Hush Little Baby • John Jacob Jingleheimer Schmidt • Oh! Susanna • On Top Of Old Smokey • Skip To My Lou • This Old Man • Three Blind Mice • more!

T2. CHRISTMAS SONGS $12.95   00102083
15 holiday favorites, including: Away In A Manger • Deck The Hall • The First Noel • Go Tell It On The Mountain • Jolly Old St. Nicholas • Joy To The World • O' Christmas Tree • O Little Town Of Bethlehem • Up On The Housetop • more!

T3. CONTEMPORARY HITS $12.95   00102099
Play with the band to eight favorite hits: Candle In The Wind • Can't Smile Without You • Kokomo • Longer • Lost In Your Eyes • Somewhere Out There • What A Wonderful World.

T4. SINGALONG FAVORITES $12.95   00102082
Everyone will enjoy these 15 classic singalongs: Bicycle Built For Two • Bill Bailey Won't You Please Come Home • Give My Regards To Broadway • Let Me Call You Sweetheart • Take Me Out To The Ballgame • When The Saints Go Marching In • much more.

T5. BROADWAY'S BEST $12.95   00102100
10 of Broadway's absolute best, including: All I Ask Of You • Don't Cry For Me Argentina • I Dreamed A Dream • Memory • Sound Of Music.

T6. COUNTRY STANDARDS $12.95   00102101
12 songs from your favorite country stars, including: I Just Fall In Love Again • Forever And Ever Amen • I Fall To Pieces • Rocky Top • Heartbreak Hotel • more.

T7. TEENAGE MUTANT NINJA TURTLES $12.95   00102111
8 radical turtle tunes from the movie sensation, including T-U-R-T-L-E Power! • Every Heart Needs A Home • Turtle Rhapsody. Also includes many full color photos from the movie itself.

SONGBOOKS

2. COUNTRY SOUND $5.95   00100374
21 country classics, including: Born To Lose • Cold, Cold Heart • Green, Green Grass Of Home • Half As Much • Hey Good Lookin' • Jambalaya • King Of The Road • Make The World Go Away • Your Cheatin' Heart.

3. TOP POPS $5.95   00100585
21 pop hits, including: Chances Are • Bye Bye Love • Candy Man • Feelings • I Want To Hold Your Hand • Music To Watch Girls By • One Tin Soldier • Paper Roses • Put Your Hand In The Hand • Ramblin' Rose.

4. DANCE BAND GREATS $5.95   00100382
21 greats, including: Fly Me To The Moon • Harbor Lights • In The Mood • Love Me Or Leave Me • Paper Doll • September Song • Side By Side • There's A Small Hotel • Things We Did Last Summer • Try To Remember.

5. ALL-TIME STANDARDS $5.95 00100305
21 standards, including: And The Angels Sing • The Bells Of St. Mary's • Everybody Loves My Baby • Harlem Nocturne • Hawaiian Wedding Song • Memories Of You • Que Sera Sera • Rain • To Love Again • Undecided • What A Diff'rence A Day Made • When I Fall In Love.

6. GIANT HITS $5.95 00100428
21 Beatles' songs, including: All My Loving • And I Love Her • Can't Buy Me Love • Eleanor Rigby • Get Back • A Hard Day's Night • Hey Jude • Let It Be • Michelle • Norwegian Wood • Yellow Submarine • Yesterday.

7. HITS FROM MUSICALS $5.95 00100442
21 hits, including: As Long As He Needs Me • How Are Things In Glocca Morra • I Could Write A Book • I've Grown Accustomed To Her Face • Gonna Build A Mountain • Manhattan • More • On A Clear Day • Summertime • Wouldn't It Be Loverly.

8. PATRIOTIC SONGS $5.95 00100490
21 tunes, including: America • America The Beautiful • Battle Hymn Of The Republic • Dixie • God Bless America • Star Spangled Banner • This Is My Country • This Land Is Your Land • Yellow Rose Of Texas • You're A Grand Old Flag.

9. CHRISTMAS TIME $5.95 00100355
21 favorites, including: Away In A Manger • Deck The Halls • The First Noel • God Rest Ye Merry Gentlemen • Hark! The Herald Angels Sing • It Came Upon A Midnight Clear • Jingle Bells • Joy To The World • O Christmas Tree • O Come All Ye Faithful • Silent Night.

10. HAWAIIAN SONGS $5.95 00100435
21 Polynesian songs, including: Aloha Oe • The Breeze And I • Hawaiian Wedding Song • The Moon Of Manakoora • Now Is The Hour • Pearly Shells • Quiet Village • Sea Breeze • Song Of The Islands • Tiny Bubbles.

11. RECORDED HITS $5.95 00100560
19 top recording hits, including: Always On My Mind • Born Free • Danke Schoen • I Believe In Music • Love Me Do • Morning Has Broken • Put Your Hand In The Hand • Spanish Eyes • Time In A Bottle.

12. DANCEABLE FAVORITES $5.95 00100386
21 songs, including: Downtown • I'll Never Smile Again • It's Not Unusual • Let It Be Me • My Love • Quiet Nights Of Ouiet Stars • Strangers In The Night • A Sunday Kind Of Love • Till Then.

13. CELEBRATED FAVORITES $5.95 00100345
21 favorites, including: Ain't Misbehavin' • For Me And My Gal • Hey, Mr. Banjo • I Can't Give You Anything But Love • I've Got The World On A String • The Sheik Of Araby • Star Dust • That's My Desire • When You're Smiling • Who's Sorry Now.

14. ALL-TIME REQUESTS $5.95 00100300
21 requests, including: April Showers • Blueberry Hill • Heartaches • I Don't Know Why • I'll Get By • I Talk To The Trees • The Old Piano Roll Blues • Too Close For Comfort • What Kind Of Fool Am I? • You Can't Be True Dear.

15. COUNTRY PICKIN'S $5.95 00100370
21 country tunes, including: Abilene • Deep In The Heart Of Texas • Hello Walls • I Can't Stop Loving You • It Wasn't God Who Made Honky Tonk Angels • My Elusive Dreams • Night Train To Memphis • Oh, Lonesome Me • Wabash Cannon Ball • Walking In The Sunshine.

16. BROADWAY'S BEST $6.95 00100335
21 show tunes, including: Bali Hai • Climb Ev'ry Mountain • Edelweiss • My Favorite Things • Oh What A Beautiful Mornin' • Some Enchanted Evening • The Sound Of Music • The Surrey With The Fringe On Top • The Sweetest Sounds • Younger Than Springtime.

17. FIRESIDE SINGALONG $5.95 00100415
24 singalongs, including: Alouette • Bicycle Built For Two • Blue Tail Fly • Clementine • For He's A Jolly Good Fellow • Hail, Hail The Gang's All Here • I Love You Truly • I've Been Working On The Railroad • My Bonnie • She'll Be Comin' 'Round The Mountain.

18. CLASSICAL PORTRAITS $5.95 00100362
21 classical themes, including: Blue Danube Waltz • Brahm's Lullaby • Fantasie Impromptu • Humoresque • Liebestraum • Poet And Peasant Overture • Reverie • Romeo And Juliet • Tales From The Vienna Woods • Vienna Life.

19. POLKA AND MARCH BEATS $5.95 00100540
21 polkas and marches, including: Barbara Polka • Clarinet Polka • Helena Polka • High School Cadets • Julida Polka • King Cotton March • Pizzacato Polka • Semper Fidelis • Sharpshooters March • Tinker Polka.

21. SINGALONG STANDARDS $5.95 00100578
21 standards, including: After The Ball • Bill Bailey, Won't You Please Come Home • Give My Regards To Broadway • Ida • In My Merry Oldsmobile • In The Good Old Summertime • Mary's A Grand Old Name • My Wild Irish Rose • Sidewalks Of New York • Sweet Adeline • Wait 'Til The Sun Shines Nellie.

22. SACRED SOUNDS $5.95 00100570
21 hymns, including: Abide With Me • Fairest Lord Jesus • Give Me That Old Time Religion • The Sweet Bye And Bye • Joshua Fit The Battle Of Jericho • Nearer, My God, To Thee • Onward Christian Soldiers • Rock Of Ages • What A Friend We Have In Jesus • Whispering Hope.

23. DISNEY SPOTLIGHTS $5.95 00100405
17 hits, including: The Ballad Of Davy Crockett • The Bare Necessities • Chim Chim Cher-ee • Never Smile At A Crocodile • Once Upon A Dream • Peter Pan • Supercalifragilisticexpialidocious • You Can Fly! You Can Fly!

24. (THE MAGIC OF) M-I-C-K-E-Y $5.95 00100480
17 selections, including: Bibbidi-Bobbidi Boo • A Dream Is A Wish Your Heart Makes • I'm Late • It's A Small World • Mickey Mouse March • No Other Love • The Unbirthday Song • Westward Ho The Wagons!

25. DISNEY DAZZLE $5.95 00100397
17 favorites, including: Give A Little Whistle • Heigh Ho,Heigh Ho • I'm Wishing • Lavender Blue • Some Day My Prince Will Come • When You Wish Upon A Star • Whistle While You Work • Who's Afraid Of The Big Bad Wolf? • Zip-A-Dee-Doo-Dah.

26. HOLLY SEASON $5.95 00100100
21 favorite Christmas songs, including: Frosty The Snowman • I Heard The Bells On Christmas Day • Jingle-Bell Rock • O Holy Night • The Twelve Days Of Christmas • We Wish You A Merry Christmas • The Christmas Waltz • My Favorite Things • Pretty Paper • Parade Of The Wooden Soldiers.

27. SONGS ABOUT GIRLS $5.95 00100190
20 unforgettable women in song, including: Carrie Ann • Charmaine • Daddy's Little Girl • Hello Mary Lou • Honeysuckle Rose • If You Knew Susie • Little Jeannie • Miss America • Second Hand Rose • Sweet Caroline.

28. 50 CLASSICAL THEMES $9.95 00101598
Beethoven Symphony No. 6 (5th Movement) • Eine Kleine Nachtmusik (14th Movement) • The Great Gate Of Kiev (From "Pictures At An Exhibition") • Grieg Piano Concerto (1st Movement) • Hungarian Rhapsody No. 2 • Largo (From "Xerxes") • Meditation (From "Thais") • Mendelssohn Violin Concerto (1st Movement) • Mozart Piano Sonata In A (3rd Movement) • Song Of India (From "Sadko") • Tchaikovsky Violin Conceno (1st Movement) • "William Tell" Overture (Closing Theme).

29. LOVE SONGS $5.95 00100135
19 romantic ballads, including: Feelings • The Glory Of Love • Hopelessly Devoted To You • Matchmaker • Shadows In The Moonlight • Sunrise, Sunset • Try To Remember • Unforgettable.

30. COUNTRY CONNECTION $5.95 00100030
20 country greats, including: Cool Water • Here I Am Drunk Again • I Don't Care • I Walk The Line • Love Me Tender • Release Me • Room Full Of Roses • Since I Met You Baby • Wooden Heart.

31. BIG BAND FAVORITES $5.95 00100010
21 all-time recording hits, including: East Of The Sun • In A Little Spanish Town • I'll Remember April • It's The Talk Of The Town • Manhattan • My Melancholy Baby • Pennies From Heaven • A String Of Pearls • Tuxedo Junction • Twelfth Of Never • Yes Indeed.

32. ROCK & COUNTRY $5.95 00100180
21 super pop hits, including: All Shook Up • Bad, Bad Leroy Brown • Do You Want To Dance? • Houston • Islands In The Stream • A Little Good News • Love Me Do • People Got To Be Free • Save The Last Dance For Me • Your Mamma Don't Dance.

33. MEMORABLE STANDARDS $5.95 00100150
20 sentimental songs, including: Calcutta • Can't Help Falling In Love • 'Deed I Do • Five Foot Two, Eyes Of Blue • Let's Dance • Mr. Wonderful • My Man • Second Hand Rose • That's All • Young At Heart.

34. COUNTRY CLASSICS $5.95 00100020
20 greats, including: Any Time • Blue Suede Shoes • Candy Kisses • Detour • Don't Rob Another Man's Castle • Dream On Little Dreamer • Heartbroke • Help Me Make It Through The Night • I Really Don't Want To Know • Sixteen Tons.

35. FAMILIAR HITS $5.95 00100055
21 assorted pops, including: Can't Smile Without You • Daddy Don't You Walk So Fast • Fever • Goodbye Yellow Brick Road • Green Door • If I Were A Carpenter • Keep On Singing • Midnight Blue • Sleepwalk • Spanish Harlem • Yellow Days.

36. SPANISH MELODIES $5.95 00100582
36. MELODIAS ESPANOLAS $5.95 00100661
21 Spanish songs, including: Adios • Brazil • El Cumbanchero • El Rancho Grande • El Relicerio • Granada • How Insensitive • LePaloma • More (Mas) • Noche de Ronda (Be Mine Tonight) • Perfidia • Tico-Tico.

37. FAVORITE LATIN SONGS $5.95 00100410
37. CANCIONES FAVORITAS $5.95 00100660
21 Spanish melodies, including: Amapola • Besame Mucho • Desafinado • Frenesi • Guadalajara • La Cumparsita • Lisbon Antigua • Maria Elena • Meditation • Quizas, Quizas, Quizas (Perhaps, Perhaps, Perhaps) • Tango Of Roses.

38. SENTIMENTAL BALLADS $5.95 00100573
21 ballads, including: April In Paris • Avalon • Days Of Wine And Roses • Indian Love Call • It Had To Be You • La Vie En Rose • My Own True Love • Secret Love • The Simple Life • (Theme From) A Summer Place • What Now My Love.

39. SONGS OF THE 20'S $5.95 00100580
21 favorites, including: April Showers • The Birth Of The Blues • Charleston • I Know That You Know • I Want To Be Happy • Sometimes I'm Happy • Stouthearted Men • Sweet Georgia Brown • Tea For Two • Tip Toe Thru' The Tulips With Me.

40. SONGS OF THE 30'S $5.95 00100581
21 songs from the 30's, including: April In Paris • As Time Goes By • My Dear • Dancing In The Dark • Fine And Dandy • I Only Have Eyes For You • Jeepers Creepers • September In The Rain • Three Little Words • When Your Love Has Gone • Zing Went The Strings Of My Heart.

41. SONGS OF GERSHWIN, PORTER, & RODGERS $5.95 00100425
21 songs, including: Anything Goes • The Blue Room • But Not For Me • Embraceable You • Fascinating Rhythm • I Got Rhythm • Oh! Lady Be Good • Somebody Loves Me • Thou Swell • What Is This Thing Called Love?

42. NOSTALGIC TUNES $5.95 00100485
21 melodies, including: Alabama Jubilee • Bei Mir Bist Du Schon • By The Light Of The Silvery Moon • It's All In The Game • Long Ago, Far Away • Mack The Knife • Puff (The Magic Dragon) •Quando, Quando, Quando • The River Seine • You Oughta Be In Pictures.

43. SINGALONG REQUESTS $5.95 00100576
21 singalong tunes, including: Ain't She Sweet • Ain't We Got Fun • Baby Face • Bye Bye Blackbird • California, Here I Come • Happy Days Are Here Again • I'm Looking Over A Four Leaf Clover • Moonlight Bay • My Heart Stood Still • Pretty Baby • Smiles.

44. THE BEST OF WILLIE NELSON $7.95 00102135
39 of his very best including: Always On My Mind • Blue Eyes Crying In The Rain • Crazy • Georgia On My Mind • Help Me Make It Through The Night • Make The World Go Away • Mammas Don't Let Your Babies Grow Up To Be Cowboys • On The Road Again • To All The Girls I've Loved Before • and more.

45. LOVE BALLADS — Double-Note Melodies $5.95 00100460
21 love songs, including: Canadian Sunset • Can't Help Lovin' Dat Man • I Will Wait For You • If I Loved You • The Last Time I Saw Paris • Little Girl Blue • Look For The Silver Lining • Lovely To Look At • Ol' Man River • This Can't Be Love • You'll Never Walk Alone.

46. HAWAIIAN FAVORITES $5.95 00100090
21 favorites, including: Beyond The Reef • Ka-Lu-A • Lovely Hula Hands • Mapuana • Mele Kalikimaka • One Paddle-Two Paddle • The Sands Of Waikiki • Songs Of The Islands • That's The Hawaiian In Me • Waikiki.

47. COUNTRY TIMES $5.95 00100376
22 favorites, including: A Broken Hearted Me • Do You Love As Good As You Look • Don't It Make Your Brown Eyes Blue • He Stopped Loving Her Today • I Believe In You • Lady • Last Cheater's Waltz • A Lesson In Leavin' • Old Flames Can't Hold A Candle To You • True Love Ways.

48. GOSPEL SONGS OF JOHNNY CASH $5.95 00100343
20 songs, including: The Great Speckled Bird • Peace In The Valley • My God Is Real • On The Jericho Road • How Great Thou Art • The Old Rugged Cross • I'll Fly Away • Will The Circle Be Unbroken • Were You There When They Crucified My Lord? • Just A Closer Walk With Thee.

49. ELVIS, ELVIS, ELVIS $7.95 00100043
21 famous Elvis hits, including: All Shook Up • Blue Suede Shoes • Can't Help Falling In Love • Don't Be Cruel • Heartbreak Hotel • Hound Dog • I Want You, I Need You, I Love You • It's Now Or Never • Jailhouse Rock • Love Me Tender • (Let Me Be Your) Teddy Bear.

50. THE BEST OF PATSY CLINE $6.95 00102114
25 of her best including Back In Baby's Arms • I Fall To Pieces • Three Cigarettes In An Ashtray • Your Cheatin' Heart • Crazy • and more.

51. SANDI PATTI ANTHOLOGY $14.95 00102121
40 of her best, including: How Majestic Is Your Name • It's Your Song Lord • Let There Be Praise • Love In Any Language • Make His Praise Glorious • More Than Wonderful • O Magnify The Lord • and more.

53. IRVING BERLIN HITS—2 $5.95 00100328
21 Irving Berlin tunes, including: Blue Skies • Count Your Blessings Instead Of Sheep • Let's Take An Old Fashioned Walk • Mandy • Marie • A Pretty Girl Is Like A Melody • Puttin' On The Ritz • Say It Isn't So • Soft Lights And Sweet Music • There's No Business Like Show Business • They Say It's Wonderful.

54. GOSPEL FAVORITES $6.95 00100431
21 songs of inspiration, including: Amazing Grace • Faith Of Our Fathers • His Name Is Wonderful • How Great Thou Art • I Expect A Miracle • Jesus Is Coming Again • Just A Closer Walk With Thee • Just As I Am • Whispering Hope • You Can Touch Him.

55. JOHNNY CASH $6.95 00100342
Includes: Folsom Prison Blues • I Walk The Line • Five Feet High And Rising • Don't Take Your Guns To Town • Daddy Sang Bass • Ragged Old Flag • San Quentin • Orange Blossom Special • Long Black Veil • Ring Of Fire • John Henry • One Piece At A Time • many more.

56. HANK WILLIAMS JR. GREATEST HITS $9.95 00102139
31 of his best including: Born To Boogie • A Country Boy Can Survive • Mind Your Own Business • There's A Tear In My Beer • Young Country • and more.

57. THE BEST OF ABBA $5.95 00101425
A collection of 20 songs recorded by ABBA, including: • Does Your Mother Know • Fernando • I Do, I Do, I Do, I Do, I Do • The Name Of The Game • SOS • Take A Chance On Me • The Winner Takes It All.

58. THE BEST OF LENNY DEE $5.95 00100329
A collection of 16 recorded hits, including: Alabamy Bound • Alley Cat Song • By The Time I Get To Phoenix • Bye Bye Blues • The Exodus Song • Georgia On My Mind • Georgy Girl • Red Roses For A Blue Lady • 'Way Down Yonder In New Orleans • Yes Sir, That's My Baby.

59. CHRISTMAS SONGS $5.95 00100353
22 songs, including: A Holly, Jolly Christmas • Home For The Holidays • I Heard The Bells On Christmas Day • I'll Be Home For Christmas • Let It Snow! Let It Snow! Let It Snow! • A Marshmallow World • Rockin' Around The Christmas Tree • Rudolph, The Red-Nosed Reindeer • Sleigh Ride • There Is No Christmas Like A Home Christmas.

60. POPS OF THE 70'S $5.95 00100173
16 songs, including: Day By Day • Everything Is Beautiful • Here Comes That Rainy Day Feeling Again • I Like Dreamin' • Knock Three Times • Maggie May • Reminiscing • Sara Smile • Stayin' Alive.

61. THE BEST OF ALABAMA $6.95 00101440
22 of their greatest, including: Alabama Sky • The Closer You Get • Dixieland Delight • Feels So Right • Lady Down On Love • Love In The First Degree • Mountain Music • Take Me Down • Why Lady Why.

62. FAVORITE HYMNS — Double Note Melodies $5.95 00100409
21 well-known hymns, including: Ave Maria • Bringing In The Sheaves • Come, Thou Almighty King • God Of Our Fathers • Holy, Holy, Holy • Jesus Loves Me! This I Know • A Mighty Fortress Is Our God • My Faith Looks up To Thee • The Old 100th Psalm • The Rosary • Stand Up! Stand Up! For Jesus.

63. CLASSICAL MUSIC (ENGLISH/SPANISH TEXT) $5.95 00100360
22 classics: Barcarolle • Clair de Lune • Czardas • Dance Of The Hours • Danube Waves • Fifth Symphony • Hungarian Dance No. 5 • Melody In F • Military Polonaise • Tannhauser March • Toccata And Fugue In D Minor • Waltz In A Minor.

64. DANCE LITTLE BIRD $5.95 00100384
Includes: Dance Little Bird • The Great Waltz • My Melody Of Love • It's A Small World • Let's All Sing Like The Birdies Sing • Nashville Beer Garden • Henrietta Polka • German Medley • Circus Fantasy • I'll Never Get Married Again • Fly Little Bird.

65. THE BEST OF THE JUDDS $5.95 00101722
15 tunes, including: Blue Nun Cafe • Change Of Heart • Cry Myself To Sleep • Don't Be Cruel • Dream Chaser • A Girl's Night Out • Grandpa (Tell Me 'Bout The Good Old Days) • If I Were You • Mama He's Crazy • Rockin' With The Rhythm Of The Rain • more.

66. COUNTRY GOLD $5.95 00100367
21 hits, including: Convoy • Country Bumpkin • Country Sunshine • The End Of The World • Every Time You Touch Me (I Get High) • Honky Tonk Wine • I Believe The South Is Gonna Rise Again • I Miss You • Kiss An Angel Good Mornin' • Look At Them Beans • (I'm A) Ramblin' Man.

67. INTERNATIONAL HITS $5.95 00100447
67. EXITOS (SPANISH TEXT) $5.95 00100666
21 international favorites, including: Alpha Oe • Alone Again (Naturally) • The Exodus Song • Fur Elise • La Paloma • La Violetera • Los Nardos • Macarena • Only You • Valencia.

68. WILLIE NELSON $5.95 00100250
21 songs, including: After The Fire Is Gone • Blue Eyes Crying In The Rain • Both Ends Of The Candle • Congratulations • Country Willie • Crazy • Healing Hands Of Time • I Gotta Get Drunk • Kneel At The Feet Of Jesus • One Day At A Time.

69. IT'S GOSPEL $5.95 00100449
21 favorites, including: Blessed Jesus • It Took A Miracle • I Want To Be More Like Jesus • I Will Serve Thee • My God Is Real (Yes, God Is Real) • Only Believe • Take My Hand, Precious Lord • There'll Be Peace In The Valley For Me • Whither Thou Goest • Will The Circle Be Unbroken.

70. GOSPEL GREATS $5.95 00100432
21 great songs, including: Did You Stop To Pray This Morning? • In The Garden • It Is Well With My Soul • Lead Me, Guide Me • To God Be The Glory • Why Me? • He • Beyond The Sunset.

71. VIENNESE WALTZES $5.95 00100595
21 songs, including: Danube Nymphs Waltz • Gold And Siver Waltz • The Merry Widow Waltz • Philomel Waltz • The Sirens • Sylvia • Tres Jolie (Charming Waltz) • Vienna Beauties • Village Swallows Waltz • Waltz, Op. 101, No. 11.

72. ELVIS PRESLEY GREATEST HITS — VOL. I $4.95 00100045
12 hit songs, including: Blue Suede Shoes • Follow That Dream • Frankie And Johnnie • G.I. Blues • Girls, Girls, Girls • Hurt • Kissin' Cousins • Love Me Tender • Wooden Heart.

73. ELVIS PRESLEY GREATEST HITS — VOL. II $4.95 00100046
12 hit songs, including: Are You Lonesome Tonight • Crying In The Chapel • Don't Be Cruel • Good Luck Charm • Kentucky Rain • Loving You • Return To Sender • My Ring Around Your Neck.

74. HYMNS OF GLORY $5.95 00100444
21 hymns, including: All Hail The Power Of Jesus' Name • Break Thou The Bread Of Life • Built On A Rock The Church Doth Stand • The Church's One Foundation • He Leadeth Me, O Blessed Thought • I Need Thee Every Hour • Leaning On The Everlasting Arms • O Worship The King, All Glorious Above • Standing On The Promises • When I Survey The Wonderous Cross.

75. SACRED MOMENTS $5.95 00100568
21 favorites, including: And Can It Be That I Should Gain • Have You Any Room For Jesus? • I Love To Tell The Story • I Sing The Mighty Pow'r Of God • Love Lifted Me • On Christ, The Solid Rock, I Stand • Rise Up, Oh Men Of God • Tell Me The Old, Old Story • There Is Power In The Blood • Wonderful Words Of Life.

76. THE SOUND OF MUSIC $4.95 00100572
7 selections from the Broadway musical.

77. MY FAIR LADY $4.95 00100489
7 selections from the Broadway musical.

78. OKLAHOMA $4.95 00100530
7 selections from the Broadway musical.

79. SOUTH PACIFIC $4.95 00100575
7 selections from the Broadway musical.

80. THE KING AND I $4.95 00100456
7 selections from the Broadway musical.

81. FRANKIE YANKOVIC POLKAS & WALTZES $5.95 00100424
15 songs, including: Beer Barrel Polka • Bye Bye My Baby • Dance, Dance, Dance • Hoop-Dee-Doo • Just Another Polka • Pennsylvania Polka • Three Yanks Polka • The "Whoop" Polka • You Are My One True Love.

82. ROMANTIC BALLADS & ONE WALTZ $5.95 00100565
25 of the best, including: But Beautiful • Don't Take Your Love From Me • Dream • I Can't Get Started • I'm Confessin' • It's The Talk Of The Town • Seems Like Old Times • Smoke Gets In Your Eyes • This Love Of Mine • Wonderful Copenhagen.

83. SWINGTIME $6.95 00100584
26 standards, including: All Of Me • Cry Me A River • Imagination • The Lady Is A Tramp • Let's Fall In Love • Lullaby Of The Leaves • Moonlight In Vermont • Swinging On A Star • These Foolish Things Remind Me Of You.

84. BALLROOM FAVORITES $6.95   00100310
25 danceables, including: Boo Hoo • Cecilia • Charley My Boy • Love Walked In • Me And My Shadow • On A Slow Boat To China • Personality • Rags To Riches • Rockin' Chair • Then I'll Be Happy.

85. THE RICKY SKAGGS SONG BOOK $6.95   00101942
Includes: Can't You Hear Me Callin' • Crying My Heart Out Over You • Don't Get Above Your Raising • Heartbroke • Highway 40 Blues • I Don't Care • I Wouldn't Change You If I Could • Waitin' For The Sun To Shine.

86. SONGS FROM MUSICALS $5.95   00100579
21 of the best, including: Anywhere I Wander • Baubles, Bangles And Beads • Heart • Hernando's Hideaway • Hey There • If I Were A Bell • Once In Love With Amy • Seventy-Six Trombones • Stranger In Paradise • Till There Was You.

87. BEATLES BEST $17.95   00100313
Over 120 songs from the "Fab Four," including: All My Loving • All You Need Is Love • Come Together • Day Tripper • Get Back • Help! • Hey Jude • Here Comes The Sun • Let It Be • Michelle • Nowhere Man • She Loves You • Ticket To Ride • Yesterday • many more.

88. GOIN' COUNTRY $6.95   00100427
23 greats, including: Another Somebody Done Somebody Wrong Song • Blessed Are The Believers • Bombed, Boozed & Busted • Crying My Heart Out Over You • Darlin' • I Loved 'Em Everyone • I Wish I Was Eighteen Again • Long Arm Of The Law • Rest Your Love On Me • What Are We Doin' In Love • Your Wife Is Cheatin' On Us Again.

89. SONGS FOR CHILDREN $6.95   00100577
31 favorites, including: Are You Sleeping • Baa, Baa Black Sheep • Blow The Man Down • Chopsticks • The Farmer In The Dell • Hickory Dickory Dock • It Ain't Gonna Rain No More • London Bridge • Mulberry Bush • Row, Row, Row Your Boat • This Old Man.

90. ELTON JOHN ANTHOLOGY $12.95   00290104
60 of his greatest including: Bennie And The Jets • Crocodile Rock • Daniel • Goodbye Yellow Brick Road • I Guess That's Why They Call It The Blues • Lucy In The Sky With Diamonds • Philadelphia Freedom • Rocket Man • Sad Songs (Say So Much) • Tiny Dancer • Your Song.

91. THE BEST OF PAUL ANKA $5.95   00100331
17 of his best, including: Diana • (You're) Having My Baby • It Doesn't Matter Anymore • Jubilation • Let Me Try Again • Lonely Boy • My Way • Puppy Love • Put Your Head On My Shoulder • You Are My Destiny.

92. FAMILIAR HYMNS $5.95   00100411
22 favorites, including: Abide, O Dearest Jesus • All Glory And Honor • Draw Us To Thee • God Bless Our Native Land • Guide Me, O Thou Great Jehovah • Holy Ghost, With Light Divine • I Thou But Suffer God To Guide Thee • Jesus Sinners Doth Receive • O God, Thou Faithful God • Take My Life And Let It Be.

93. COUNTRY HITS $8.95   00100036
44 giants, including: By The Time I Get To Phoenix • Chains Of Love • Daddy Don't You Walk So Fast • Help Me Make It Through The Night • If I Had A Cheating Heart • Lucille • Mammas Don't Let Your Babies Grow Up To Be Cowboys • Miracles • Nobody Likes Sad Songs • Overnight Sensation • The Pittsburgh Stealers • Running Bear • A Tear Fell • Two Less Lonely People • Why Me? • Y'All Come Back Saloon.

94. JOYOUS CHRISTMAS $5.95   00100450
21 songs, including: The Angels And The Shepherds • As Lately We Watched • A Babe Is Born • All Of A Maid • Blessed Be That Maid Marie • The Boar's Head Carol • A Child This Day Is Born • Christians Awake • The Holly And The Ivy • Infant So Gentle • Once In Royal David's City.

95. JULIO IGLESIAS (SPANISH TEXT) $5.95   00100451
16 of his best, including: A Veces Tu, A Veces Yo • Abrazame • Cantandole Al Mar • Chiquilla • Como el Alamo al Camino • Cuando Vuelva-a Amanecer • Dejala • Desdeque Tu Te Has Ido • Dieciseis Anos.

96. OAK RIDGE BOYS GREATEST HITS — VOLUMES 1 & 2 $7.95   00101819
20 songs, including: American Made • Dream On • Elvira • Fancy Free • Love Song • Sail Away • Thank God For Kids • Y'All Come Back Saloon • You're The One.

97. COUNTRY PLEASURE $5.95   00100372
23 hits, including: All I Have To Do Is Dream • Dang Me • Heartbreaker • I'm Knee Deep In Loving You • It Don't Feel Like Sinnin' To Me • Middle Age Crazy • Mississippi Woman • One Piece At A Time • Stand By Your Man • There Ain't No Good Chain Gang • Womanhood.

98. STAGE & SCREEN $5.95   00101950
21 greats, including: Hello Young Lovers • I Enjoy Being A Girl • Love, Look Away • A Fellow Needs A Girl • No Other Love • People Will Say We're In Love • A Wonderful Guy • There's Nothin' Like A Dame • We Kiss In A Shadow • You Are Beautiful.

100. WINTER WONDERLAND $5.95   00100602
15 all-time favorites, including: All I Want For Christmas Is My Two Front Teeth • Christmas Auld Lang Syne • Deck The Halls • Joy To The World • The Only Thing I Want For Christmas • What Did I Say To Old St. Nick? • When It's Christmas On The Range • Winter Wonderland.

101. ANNIE $5.95   00100000
14 songs from the Broadway musical.

102. JIM CROCE — PHOTOGRAPHS & MEMORIES $5.95   00101560
14 songs from the LP, including: Bad, Bad Leroy Brown • I Got A Name • I'll Have To Say I Love You In A Song • Operator • Time In A Bottle • You Don't Mess Around With Jim • Workin' At The Car Wash Blues.

103. THE VERY BEST OF LEE GREENWOOD $7.95   00100592
19 of his best, including: God Bless The U.S.A. • Going Going Gone • I Don't Mind The Thorns (If You're The Rose) • I.O.U. • It Turns Me Inside Out • Love Song • Somebody's Gonna Love You • The Wind Beneath My Wings.

104. BOB RALSTON—BROADWAY MEMORIES $5.95   00101544
17 of his favorites, including: Bewitched • Edelweiss • Getting To Know You • I Could Have Danced All Night • If Ever I Would Leave You • My Favorite Things • Oklahoma • People Will Say We're In Love • Sunrise, Sunset.

105. THE BEST OF SIMON AND GARFUNKEL $7.95   00101928
20 of their best, including: Bridge Over Troubled Water • Cecilia • El Condor Pasa • The 59th Street Bridge Song (Feelin' Groovy) • Homeward Bound • Mrs. Robinson • Scarborough Fair • The Sound Of Silence.

106. BARBRA STREISAND—MEMORIES $6.95   00101958
The 10 songs from the LP: Coming In And Out Of Your Life • Evergreen • Lost Inside Of You • The Love Inside • Memory • My Heart Belongs To Me • New York State Of Mind • No More Tears • The Way We Were • You Don't Bring Me Flowers.

107. THE BEST OF BOB RALSTON $5.95   00101515
21 favorites, including: All The Things You Are • Have You Ever Been Lonely • If Ever I Would Leave You • I Left My Heart In San Francisco • My Prayer • Twilight Time • Watch What Happens • When My Baby Smiles At Me • World Is Waiting For The Sunrise • Yesterdays.

108. CLASSICAL THEMES (ENGLISH/SPANISHTEXT) $6.95   00100363
18 favorites, including: Ave Maria • Barcarole • Fur Elise • Hallelujah Chorus • Jesu, Joy Of Man's Desiring • Liebestraum • Minuet In G • Moonlight Sonata • Theme From Swan Lake • Unfinished Symphony.

110. THE NEIL DIAMOND COLLECTION $9.95   00101566
44 of his best, including: America • Cracklin' Rosie • Forever In Blue Jeans • Heartlight • Hello Again • Longfellow Serenade • Love On The Rocks • September Morn • Song Sung Blue • Sweet Caroline • Yesterday's Songs • You Don't Bring Me Flowers.

111. THE GREAT AMERICAN MOVIE SONGBOOK $12.95   00101611
47 all-time movie greats, including: All The Way • As Time Goes By • The Blue Room • Days Of Wine And Roses • Embraceable You • Everybody's Talkin' • The High And The Mighty • High Hopes • I Only Have Eyes For You • My Own True Love • New York, New York • Secret Love • September In The Rain • Someone To Watch Over Me • The Summer Knows • 'S Wonderful • Thou Swell • Time After Time • Where Is Your Heart • You Make Me Feel So Young.

112. THE BEST OF THE BEATLES $12.95   00101498
89 songs in over 200 pages, including: All My Loving • Day Tripper • Penny Lane • And I Love Her • Eight Days A Week • A Hard Day's Night • Help! • Norwegian Wood • Michelle • Ticket To Ride • Yesterday • Eleanor Rigby • Yellow Submarine • When I'm Sixty-Four • Hey Jude • Let It Be.

113. SONGS OF DEVOTION $5.95   00101945
21 sacred favorites, including: Alleluia • Born Again • His Name Is Wonderful • How Great Thou Art • I've Never Seen The Righteous Forsaken • If My People • Spread A Little Love Around • Sweet, Sweet Spirit • There Is One • Through It All.

114. JOYOUS GOSPEL $5.95   00101720
20 gospel greats, including: I Believe • The Lord Is My Shepherd • Make My Life A Prayer To You • Near The Cross • The Old Rugged Cross • Oh God, Our Help In Ages Past • Praise God, From Whom All Blessings Flow • Sing Hallelujah • We Gather To Ask The Lord's Blessing • With God All Things Are Possible.

115. THE GREATEST WALTZES $8.95   00101612
37 waltzes, including: Allegheny Moon • The Blue Skirt Waltz • Edelweiss • Falling In Love With Love • Fascination • I'll Take Romance • It's A Grand Night For Singing • Let Me Call You Sweetheart • Melody Of Love • My Favorite Things • Oh, What A Beautiful Mornin' • Tennessee Waltz • True Love • Wunderbar • You Can't Be True Dear.

116. DON HO SONG BOOK $6.95   00100407
30 favorites, including: Aloha • The Far Lands • Hawaiian Guitar • Here Is Happiness • Keanani • Luau Song • Maui Waltz • Moya • My Lovely Lei • Our Love And Aloha • Pearly Shells • Puka Shells • Tania • This Is Paradise • Tiny Bubbles.

117. WILLIE NELSON—JUST PLAIN WILLIE $7.95   00101725
37 songs, including 28 unreleased songs, plus these 9 bonus songs: Always On My Mind • Blue Eyes Crying In The Rain • Crazy • I'm Gonna Sit Right Down And Write Myself A Letter • Mammas Don't Let Your Babies Grow Up To Be Cowboys • My Heroes Have Always Been Cowboys • Star Dust • Up Against The Wall Red-Neck • Without A Song.

118. THE SONGS OF PAUL MCCARTNEY $5.95   00101946
20 of his best, including: Band On The Run • Good Night Tonight • Jet • Let 'Em In • Listen To What The Man Said • Live And Let Die • Mull Of Kintyre • My Love • Silly Love Songs • With A Little Luck.

119. 57 SUPER HITS $10.95   00101990
Includes: Autumn Leaves • The Christmas Song • Dinah • Enjoy Yourself • Five Minutes More • Hello Dolly! • Mister Sandman • One • Peggy Sue • Put On A Happy Face • Real Live Girl • Sentimental Journey • S'posin' • Tenderly • Vaya Con Dios • and many more.

120. THE GOSPEL SONGS OF BILL AND GLORIA GAITHER $9.95   00100433
50 of their best, including: Because He Lives • Created In His Image • Even So, Lord Jesus, Come • Get All Excited • He Touched Me • I've Been To Calvary • Jesus, I Believe What You Said • Precious Jesus • The Family Of God • This Is The Day That The Lord Hath Made.

121. BOOGIES, BLUES AND RAGS $5.95   00100333
20 greats, including: Basin Street Blues • Bugle Call Rag • A Good Man Is Hard To Find • King Porter Stomp • Man That Got Away • Maple Leaf Rag • The Original Boogie Woogie • Pine Top's Boogie • Stormy Weather • Sugar Foot Stomp.

122. THE BEST OF GILBERT AND SULLIVAN $6.95   00102123
20 of their best from the shows: The Sorcerer • H.M.S. Pinafore • The Pirates Of Penzance • Patience • Lolanthe • The Mikado • The Yeoman Of The Guard • The Gondoliers.

123. 58 SUPER HITS $10.95   00101991
Includes: Best Things In Life Are Free • Bewitched • Candy • Carioca • Dream A Little Dream Of Me • A Foggy Day • How High The Moon • I Love Paris • Lilli Marlene • Mood Indigo • Old Devil Moon • Small World • Sugar Blues • That's Entertainment • That's Life • The Way You Look Tonight • Who? • and many more.

124. COUNTRY CHRISTMAS $5.95   00101559
26 favorites, including: Blue Christmas • Christmas California • Didn't He Shine • Hard Candy Christmas • It's Christmas • Little One • Old Toy Trains • Pretty Paper • Tennessee Christmas.

125. BURNIN' COUNTRY $5.95   00100017
23 giants, including: All The Gold In California • Broken Lady • Burning Love • Dreams Of The Everyday Housewife • Duelin' Banjos • God Made Love • Help Me • A Rainy Night In Georgia • The River's Too Wide • Too Many Rivers • Up Against The Wall Red-Neck • You Decorated My Life.

126. BEST OF BARRY MANILOW $8.95   00101497
24 of this superstar's best. Songs include: Can't Smile Without You • Copacabana • Even Now • I Write The Songs • Mandy • Memory • This One's For You • Trying' To Get The Feeling Again • more.

127. JOHN DENVER'S GREATEST HITS $8.95   00101563
23 of this pop superstar's greatest, including: Annie's Song • Back Home Again • My Sweet Lady • Rocky Mountain High • Sunshine On My Shoulders • more.

128. NEIL DIAMOND'S GREATEST HITS $5.95   00100394
19 songs including: Beautiful Noise • Forever In Blue Jeans • I Am, I Said • Kentucky Woman • Play Me • Rosemary's Wine • Shilo • Solitary Man • Soolaimon • Sweet Caroline • You Don't Bring Me Flowers.

129. THE BEST OF NEIL DIAMOND $5.95   00100393
19 songs, including: Brooklyn Roads • Cherry, Cherry • Cracklin' Rosie • Desiree • Holly Holy • Longfellow Serenade • Porcupine Pie • September Morn • Song Sung Blue • Stones.

130. ROCK 'N ROLL IS HERE TO STAY $7.95   00100563
26 songs, including: Back In The U. S. A. • Bo Diddley • Great Balls Of Fire • Johnny B. Goode • Long Tall Sally • Mabelline • Rip It Up • Rock & Roll Music • Roll Over Beethoven • Shake, Rattle And Roll • Sh-Boom • Silhouettes • Stagger Lee • Surfin' U. S. A.

131. GOSPEL ALIVE $5.95   00100434
21 songs, including: All You Need • Evidence • Filled To Overflowing • Got To Tell Somebody • He Was There All The Time • I Will Praise Him • I'm Not What I Want To Be • I've Been Changed • Jesus Keeps Taking Me Higher • Second Hand Faith.

132. SONGS OF LOVE $5.95   00101944
24 songs, including: Anniversary Song • Bridal Chorus • Could I Have This Dance • Endless Love • I Love You Truly • If I Loved You • Let Me Call You Sweetheart • True Love • Wedding March • When I Fall In Love • You Needed Me.

133. GOIN' HOME TO GOSPEL $5.95   00100429
24 songs, including: Almost Home • At The Foot Of The Cross • Free At Last • His Hands • How Big Is God • I Just Came To Praise The Lord • Just The Name Jesus • Love Is The Reason • Teach Me, Lord, To Wait • You Must Be Born Again.

134. THAT CHRISTMAS FEELING $5.95   00100586
20 songs, including: Christmas Is... • The Christmas Song • Frosty The Snow Man • Gesu Bambino • It's Beginning To Look Like Christmas • Jingle Bell Rock • Little Drummer Boy • Mele Kalikimaka • The Star Carol • We Need A Little Christmas.

135. ALFRED BURT CAROLS $5.95   00100338
His14 most famous, including: Caroling, Caroling • Christmas Cometh Caroling • Come, Dear Children • Jesu Parvule (Poor Little Jesus) • O Hearken Ye • Some Children See Him • The Star Carol • We'll Dress The House • What Are The Signs.

136. RUNNIN' COUNTRY $5.95   00100566
26 hits, including: Almost Persuaded • Cotton-Eyed Joe • El Paso • Faded Love • Folsom Prison Blues • Gone • Hopelessly Devoted To You • I Almost Lost My Mind • Take Me To Your World • Wake Up Little Susie • Walking The Floor Over You.

137. THE JAZZ SINGER (NEIL DIAMOND) $6.95   00100445
Matches the LP. 16 songs, including: America • Havah Nagilah • Hello Again • Hey Louise • Jerusalem • Kol Nidre • Love On The Rocks • On The Robert E. Lee • Shabbat Shalom • Summerlove • You Baby.

139. THE BEST OF JEROME KERN $6.95   00101732
26 of Kern's greatest compositions, including: All The Things You Are • Can't Help Lovin' Dat Man • Last Time I Saw Paris • Ol' Man River • Smoke Gets In Your Eyes • Why Do I Love You? • more.

140. THE BEST OF GEORGE STRAIT $6.95   00101956
20 songs, including: The Chair • Does Fort Worth Ever Cross Your Mind • The Fireman • I'm Satisfied With You • Let's Fall To Pieces Together • Right Or Wrong • You Look So Good In Love.

141. ALL-TIME LATIN FAVORITES $5.95   00100290
17 songs, including: Call Me • The Girl From Ipanema • Green Eyes • My Shawl • One Note Samba • Perhaps, Perhaps, Perhaps • Poinciana • Return To Me • So Nice (Summer Samba) • Yellow Bird.

142. 59 SUPER HITS $9.95   00101992
Includes: Allegheny Moon • Boogie Woogie Bugle Boy • Early Autumn • For All We Know • I'll Take Romance • It's Only A Paper Moon • Little Girl • Love Is A Simple Thing • Memories • People • She • Stay With Me • Swedish Rhapsody • Unchained Melody • When Irish Eyes Are Smiling • Willow Weep For Me • Yearning • more.

143. THE BEST OF POLICE $7.95   00101860
22 of their greatest, including: De Do Do Do, De Da Da Da • Don't Stand So Close To Me • Every Breath You Take • Every Little Thing She Does Is Magic • King Of Pain • Message In A Bottle • Roxanne • Spirits In The Material World • Wrapped Around Your Finger.

144. THE BEST OF PETER, PAUL AND MARY $6.95   00101856
20 classics, including: A Soalin' • All My Trials • Blowin' In The Wind • Early Mornin' Rain • I Dig Rock And Roll Music • If I Had A Hammer • Leaving On A Jet Plane • Man Of Constant Sorrow • Puff (The Magic Dragon).

145. TOP COUNTRY SONGS $6.95   00100588
26 greats, including: Born To Be With You • Can't Help Falling In Love • (Ghost) Riders In The Sky • Good Times • (I'm Gonna) Put You Back On The Rack • It's Now Or Never • Moonlight Gambler • Sioux City Sue • Some Days Are Diamonds • True Love Ways • You Call Everybody Darling • You Don't Know Me.

146. HANK WILLIAMS—HIS BEST $7.95   00100597
26 of his biggest, including: Cold, Cold Heart • Countryfied • Hey, Good Lookin' • Honky Tonk Blues • I Can't Help It (If I'm Still In Love With You) • I Saw The Light • I'm So Lonesome I Could Cry • Jambalaya (On The Bayou) • Kaw-Liga • A Mansion On The Hill • My Son Calls Another Man Daddy • Ramblin' Man • You Win Again • Your Cheatin' Heart.

147. FOLK SONGS OF ENGLAND, SCOTLAND & IRELAND $6.95   00100420
44 song favorites, including: The Foggy, Foggy Dew • John Peel • Lincolnshire Poacher • The Noble Duke Of York • Sally In Our Alley • The Vicar Of Bray • Afton Water • Annie Laurie • The Blue Bells Of Scotland • Bonny Mary Of Argyle • Comin' Thru The Rye • Lock Lomond • My Love Is Like A Red Red Rose • Scotland The Brave • Wi' A Hundred Pipers • Come Back To Erin • The Dear Little Shamrock • Kathleen Mavourneen • Kilarney • St. Patrick Was A Gentleman • The Wearin' O' The Green.

148. BARBRA STREISAND—ONE VOICE $5.95   00101960
Matching folio to the smash live LP from Streisand—her first live performance in twenty years. 12 songs, including: Evergreen • It's A New World • Over The Rainbow • Papa, Can You Hear Me? • Somewhere • (The) Way We Were.

149. ENDLESS LOVE & OTHER GREAT LOVE SONGS $6.95   00100406
32 greats, including: Coming In And Out Of Your Life • Endless Love • Falling In Love With Love • Feelings • If This Isn't Love • Love Is Here To Stay • Loving You • Melody Of Love • My Funny Valentine • Nevertheless • September Morn • So In Love • Till • Till We Two Are One.

150. THE BEST BIG BAND SONGS EVER $14.95   00101548
69 of the greatest Big Band songs of all time, including: Ballin' The Jack • Basin Street Blues • Boogie Woogie Bugle Boy • The Continental • Don't Get Around Much Anymore • In The Mood • Opus One • Satin Doll • Sentimental Journey • String Of Pearls.

151. THE BEST OF MARVIN HAMLISCH $5.95   00101643
17 tunes, including: The Way We Were • Theme From Ice Castles • Nobody Does It Better • What I Did For Love • more.

152. THE BEST OF BUDDY HOLLY $6.95   00101550
More than 19 of his greatest, including: It's So Easy • Maybe Baby • Peggy Sue • That'll Be The Day.

153. HELLO DOLLY! $5.95   00100438
10 selections from the Broadway musical.

155. THE BEST OF BILLY JOEL $7.95   00101549
17 of his greatest, including: Allentown • Honesty • It's Still Rock And Roll To Me • Just The Way You Are • The Longest Time • Only The Good Die Young • Piano Man • She's Always A Woman To Me • Tell Her About It • Uptown Girl.

156. NEW GRAMMY AWARDS SONG OF THE YEAR $10.95   00101613
An updated edition that features every song named Grammy awards "Song Of The Year" from 1958-1988. 32 songs, including: Volare • Moon River • The Shadow Of Your Smile • Up, Up And Away • Bridge Over Troubled Water • You've Got A Friend • Killing Me Softly With His Song • The Way We Were • You Light Up My Life • Evergreen • Sailing • Bette Davis Eyes • We Are The World • That's What Friends Are For • Somewhere Out There • Don't Worry Be Happy.

157. 58 SUPER COUNTRY HITS $10.95   00100587
Includes: Another Honky Tonk Night On Broadway • Any Which Way You Can • Charlotte's Web • Cow Patti • Cowboys And Clowns • Crying My Heart Over You • Honky Tonk Man • I Just Fall In Love Again • It's Hard To Be Humble • Mountain Of Love • Ruby • Don't Take Your Love To Town.

158. THE JOHN LENNON COLLECTION $6.95   00101769
15 of his best, including: Give Peace A Chance • Imagine • Instant Karma • Mind Games • (Just Like) Starting Over • Watching The Wheels • Woman.

159. CATS $6.95   00101551
10 songs from this spectacular show, including the award-winning "Memory."

160. 60 SUPER HITS $12.95   00101993
Includes: Bandstand Boogie • Count Every Star • Daddy's Little Girl • Edelweiss • Five Foot Two, Eyes Of Blue • Gigi • I'll Remember April • It Might As Well Be Spring • My Heart Belongs To Me • Never On Sunday • She Loves You • The Third Man Theme • Too Young • Where Or When • Young At Heart • and more.

161. 61 SUPER HITS $12.95 00101994
Includes: Among My Souvenirs • Come Back To Me • The First Time Ever I Saw Your Face • From This Moment On • I Left My Heart In San Francisco • I'll Be Seeing You • If I Ruled The World • In The Still Of The Night • Just In Time • My Funny Valentine • Old Cape Cod • String Of Pearls • Through The Years • many more.

162. HITS OF THE 80'S—VOL. I $7.95 00101658
22 hits, including: America • Coming In And Out Of Your Life • Endless Love • It's Now Or Never • Love On The Rocks • Making Love • Memory • Morning Train • Ordinary People (Theme) • Through The Years • Yesterday's Songs.

163. SUPER MOVIE SONGS $8.95 00102125
25 movie hits, including: Against All Odds • Axel F • Almost Paradise • The Greatest Love Of All • I Just Called To Say I Love You • Take My Breath Away • Up Where We Belong • and more.

164. THE BEST CHRISTMAS SONGBOOK $6.95 00101530
30 all-time favorites, including: Coventry Carol • Deck The Halls • Frosty The Snowman • God Rest Ye Merry Gentlemen • Hark! The Herald Angels Sing • The Holly And The Ivy • I Heard The Bells On Christmas Day • I Saw Three Ships • Rudolph, The Red-Nosed Reindeer • Silent Night • We Wish You A Merry Christmas • Little Drummer Boy • Once In Royal David's City.

165. THE RODGERS & HAMMERSTEIN SONGBOOK $8.95 00101895
37 songs from these shows: Carousel • Flower Drum Song • The King And I • Me And Juliet • Oklahoma! • Pipe Dream • South Pacific • The Sound Of Music • State Fair.

166. THE NOVELTY SONGBOOK $9.95 00101809
34 fun-filled favorites, including: Chickery Chick • Chiquita Banana • Collegiate • Dance Little Bird • Hello Mudduh, Hello Fadduh! • The Hut-Sut Song • I Scream, You Scream — We All Scream For Ice Cream • I'm A Lonely Little Petunia • Itsy Bitsy, Teenie Weenie Yellow Polkadot Bikini • Mairzy Doats • Monster Mash • Na Na Hey Hey Kiss Him Goodbye • Open The Door, Richard! • Purple People Eater • Rag Mop • Little Fishies • Yes! We Have No Bananas

167. THE MICKEY GILLEY SONGBOOK $7.95 00101792
29 of his best, including: Bouquet Of Roses • Chains Of Love • City Lights • Faded Love • Lawdy Miss Clawdy • Lonely Nights • The More I Turn The Bottle Up • Overnight Sensation • The Power Of Positive Drinkin' • Room Full Of Roses • Stand By Me • True Love Ways • You Don't Know Me.

168. BARBRA STREISAND — THE BROADWAY ALBUM $6.95 00101959
All of the songs from the smash hit album, featuring: Somewhere • If I Loved You • Can't Help Lovin' That Man.

169. HITS OF THE 60'S, 70'S & 80'S $10.95 00101656
46 of the top songs from the last three decades. Songs include: And When I Die • Dust In The Wind • Fire And Rain • Holding Back The Years • I'm So Excited • Just The Way You Are • Longer • Physical • Rock On • Spinning Wheel • Stoney End • Venus • Wild Thing • With Or Without You • more.

170. THE BEST OF KENNY ROGERS $9.95 00101900
16 of his best, including: Coward Of The County • The Gambler • Love The World Away • Reuben James • Ruby • She Believes In Me • A Love Song.

171. THE BEST OF ELTON JOHN $5.95 00101537
15 songs, including: Blue Eyes • Crocodile Rock • Daniel • Don't Let The Sun Go Down On Me • Goodbye Yellow Brick Road • Rocket Man • Someone Saved My Life Tonight • Sorry Seems To Be The Hardest Word • Your Song.

172. THE MUSIC MAN $4.95 00101796
8 selections from the Broadway musical.

173. THE COMPLETE WEDDING SONGBOOK $10.95 00101558
28 songs of love, including: Anniversary Song • Endless Love • Feelings • Hawaiian Wedding Song • If We Only Have Love • Love Me Tender • Through The Years • Till True Love • Try To Remember • Wedding March • You Needed Me.

174. PHIL COLLINS - MORE GREATEST HITS $6.95 00102136
16 of the best from this pop superstar, including: Against All Odds • Another Day In Paradise • I Don't Care anymore • I Wish It Would Rain Down • In The Air Tonight • One More Night • Something Happened On The Way To Heaven • Take Me Home • Tonight, Tonight, Tonight • and more.

175. THE BEST OF DAN FOGELBERG $6.95 00101603
15 of his greatest hits, including: Hard To Say • Leader Of The Band • Longer • Part Of The Plan • Power Of Gold • Same Old Lang Syne • Twins Theme.

176. THE MICHEL LEGRAND SONGBOOK $10.95 00101755
40 of his best, including: Brian's Song (The Hands Of Time) • The Summer Knows (Summer of '42) • The Windmills Of Your Mind • The Way He Makes Me Feel.

177. FIDDLER ON THE ROOF $5.95 00101592
11 songs from the Broadway musical.

178. OLIVER! $4.95 00101825
13 titles from the Broadway musical.

179. THE BEST OF HUEY LEWIS & THE NEWS $6.95 00101665
13 of their greatest hits, including: The Heart Of Rock And Roll • Hip To Be Square • I Want A New Drug • If This Is It • Jacob's Ladder • The Power Of Love.

180. THE BEST OF LIONEL RICHIE $9.95 00101773
21 of his greatest hits, including: All Night Long (All Night) • Dancing On The Ceiling • Endless Love • Hello • Running With The Night • Say You, Say Me • Stuck On You • Truly.

181. THE GREAT AMERICAN COUNTRY SONGBOOK $12.95 00101610
70 songs, including: Any Day Now • By The Time I Get To Phoenix • Cold, Cold Heart • Crackers • Darlin' • Daytime Friends • El Paso • Every Which Way But Loose • Heartbroke • Honey • I Don't Care • I Love • I Walk The Line • I Wouldn't Have Missed It For The World • It Was Almost Like A Song • It's A Heartache • It's Hard To Be Humble • Jambalaya (On The Bayou) • Little Green Apples • Luckenbach, Texas • Miracles • Rocky Top • Smoky Mountain Rain • Somebody's Knockin' • Stand By Me • Stand By Your Man • Swingin' • Your Cheatin' Heart.

182. MICHAEL JACKSON — BAD $6.95 00101694
Matching folio to the smash hit LP. Features the songs: Bad • The Way You Make Me Feel • Man In The Mirror • I Just Can't Stop Loving You.

183. 63 SUPER HITS $12.95 00101996
Includes: Calcutta • Charmaine • Day By Day • 'Deed I Do • Fever • Green Door • Happy Together • Indiana • Lady • Love Will Keep Us Together • Memory • Midnight Blue • Mr. Wonderful • My Coloring Book • That's All , Till Tomorrow • Up, Up And Away • What A Wonderful World • Your Song • and more.

184. MERLE HAGGARD ANTHOLOGY $10.95 00290252
49 of this country superstar's biggest hits, including: From Graceland To The Promised Land • It's Not Love (But It's Not Bad) • The Legend Of Bonnie and Clyde • Me And Crippled Soldiers • Okie From Muskogee • A Place To Fall Apart • You Take Me For Granted.

185. MICHAEL JACKSON—THRILLER $6.95 00101693
10 songs from the LP.

186. 40 POP & ROCK SONG CLASSICS $12.95 00101606
Includes: Goodbye Girl • A Horse With No Name • Hotel California • The Hustle • I Believe In Music • If • Margaritaville • On Broadway • Rhinestone Cowboy • The Rose • Southern Nights • Star Wars (Main Theme) • Take It To The Limit • Time In A Bottle • Tin Man • We Are Family • Welcome Back • more.

187. 40 TOP HITS OF THE 80'S $12.95 00101607
Africa • Arthur's Theme • Billy Jean • Can You Read My Mind? • Chariots Of Fire • Escape (The Pina Colada Song) • Even Now • Eye Of The Tiger • Him • I've Got A Rock And Roll Heart • Mountain Music • Nine To Five • This Is It • Up Where We Belong • You Decorated My Life • Sailing • and more.

188. 64 STANDARD HITS $12.95 00101997
64 standards, including: The Breeze And I • The Exodus Song • Flashdance . . . What A Feeling • God : Bless The Child • If Ever I Would Leave You • Islands In The Stream • Manhattan Memory • More • Moonlight Serenade • Paper Doll • September Song • Song Sung Blue • Song Of The Islands • Summertime • Three Coins In A Fountain •Total Eclipse Of The Heart • Try To Remember • What A Diff'rence A Day Made • You Don't Bring Me Flowers • Yours • more.

190. 17 SUPER CHRISTMAS HITS $5.95 00101939
Including: The Christmas Song • The Christmas Waltz • Frosty The Snowman • I Heard The Bells On Christmas Day • I'll Be Home For Christmas • It's Beginning To Look Like Christmas • The Little Drummer Boy • Rudolph, The Red-Nosed Reindeer • Sleigh Ride • We Need A Little Christmas.

191. POPS OF THE 60'S & 70'S $10.95 00101865
39 hits, including: Baby Don't Get Hooked On Me • Breaking Up Is Hard To Do • Go Away, Little Girl • I Feel The Earth Move • If • Leader Of The Pack • Mr. Bojangles • Mr. Tambourine Man • One Fine Day • Stairway To Heaven • You've Got A Friend.

192. 65 STANDARD HITS $14.95 00101998
Includes: Begin The Beguine • Blues In The Night • Body And Soul • Brian's Song • Dancing In The Dark • Hooray For Hollywood • I Only Have Eyes For You • The Look Of Love • Love Me Or Leave Me • Misty • New York, New York • On Broadway • Paloma Blanca • Put Your Hand In The Hand • The Rose • Softly As In A Morning Sunrise • Spanish Eyes • There's A Kind Of Hush • Wonderland By Night • You Do Something To Me • and more.

193. 66 STANDARD HITS $14.95 00101999
Includes: Ain't She Sweet • Autumn In New York • Born Free • The High and The Mighty • Gotta Right To Sing The Blues • Just One Of Those Things • L-O-V-E • Let's Fly Away • Liza • Song From M*A*S*H • The More I See You • Near You • Night And Day • Nine To Five • Poor Butterfly • Skylark • Snowbird • Sweet Georgia Brown • What's New • and more.

194. 67 STANDARD HITS $14.95 00101941
Includes: Always On My Mind • April In Paris • Bye Bye Blackbird • Dream • If • Java Jive • Jean • Lullaby Of Broadway • Theme From Mahogany • The Man I Love • Nadia's Theme (The Young And The Restless) • September In The Rain • Serenade In Blue • Smiles • Strike Up The Band • Tea For Two • Time After Time • A Time For Love • The Way We Were • What Is This Thing Called Love • and more.

195. THE BEST OF COLE PORTER $6.95 00101870
23 of his greatest, including: Anything Goes • Begin The Beguine • I Get A Kick Out Of You • Just One Of Those Things • Let's Do It (Let's Fall In Love) • Love For Sale • Night And Day • What Is This Thing Called Love? • You Do Something To Me.

196. THE BEST OF GEORGE GERSHWIN $7.95 00101609
27 of his greatest, including: Bidin' My Time • But Not For Me • Embraceable You • Fascinating Rhythm • I Got Rhythm • The Man I Love • 'S Wonderful • Somebody Loves Me • Someone To Watch Over Me • Swanee.

198. COUNTRY HITS OF THE 80'S $5.95 00101561
20 contemporary hits, including: Baby I Lied • Don't Cheat In Our Hometown • Honey (Open The Door) • Islands In The Stream • Just A Little Love • A Little Good News • Personally • Why Not Me.

199. JUMBO SONGBOOK $19.95   00100453
274 songs for all occasions: College Songs • American Patriotic Songs • Humorous Songs • International Folk Songs • Classical Themes • Hymns And Sacred Songs • Latin Songs • Operetta Themes • Polkas And Marches • Waltzes • Singalongs • Children's Songs • Songs Of Christmas • Wedding Music.

200. THE BEST SONGS EVER $16.95   00101539
75 of the best E-Z Play Today songs, including: Edelweiss • Endless Love • Feelings • The Hawaiian Wedding Song • Here's That Rainy Day • I Left My Heart In San Francisco • Let It Be Me • Love Is Blue • Memory • Misty • More • My Funny Valentine • My Way • People • Satin Doll • Send In The Clowns • Smile • Star Dust • Summertime • Sunrise, Sunset • True Love • TryTo Remember • You Needed Me.

201. THE RICHARD CLAYDERMAN SONGBOOK $5.95   00101555
13 hits, including: Ballade Pour Adeline • Feelings • Hello • Lara's Theme • Love Is Blue • Love Story • Memory • Moon River.

202. THE BEST COUNTRY SONGS EVER $14.95   00101540
70 songs, including: Always On My Mind • Any Day Now • Baby I Lied • Behind Closed Doors • Crazy • Crying In The Chapel • Funny How Time Slips Away • Green Green Grass Of Home • Heartaches By The Number • I Wish I Was Eighteen Again • Islands In The Stream • It Was Almost Like A Song • It's A Heartache • Jambalaya (On The Bayou) • King Of The Road • A Little Good News • Little Green Apples • Luckenbach, Texas • Make The World Go Away • Rhinestone Cowboy • Rocky Top • Smoky Mountain Rain • Walking In The Sunshine • Walking The Floor Over You • You Put The Beat In My Heart • Your Cheatin' Heart.

203. THE BEST BROADWAY SONGS EVER $14.95   00101541
73 songs, including: All The Things You Are • As Long As He Needs Me • Bewitched • Cabaret • Camelot • Don't Cry For Me Argentina • Everything's Coming Up Roses • Falling In Love With Love • Hello, Young Lovers • I Could Have Danced All Night • If Ever I Would Leave You • If I Loved You • It Might As Well Be Spring • Just In Time • The Lady Is A Tramp • Make Believe • My Funny Valentine • Oklahoma • Ol' Man River • On The Street Where You Live • People • Send In The Clowns • September Song • Summertime • Till There Was You • What Kind Of Fool Am I?

204. THE BEST EASY LISTENING SONGS EVER $14.95   00101542
76 songs, including: Around The World • By The Time I Get To Phoenix • Careless Whisper • Come In From The Rain • Come Rain Or Come Shine • Cry Me A River • Day By Day • Don't Cry Out Loud • Every Breath You Take • A Foggy Day • The Girl From Ipanema • God Bless The Child • I Will Wait For You • I Wouldn't Have Missed It For The World • I'll Never Smile Again • Last Time I Saw Paris • Long Ago And Far Away • Love Is Blue • Manhattan • Midnight Blue • More • My Way • On A Clear Day • Song Sung Blue • Strangers In The Night • They Can't Take That Away From Me • You Don't Bring Me Flowers.

205. THE BEST LOVE SONGS EVER $14.95   00101543
70 giant songs, including: Can't Help Falling In Love • Can't Smile Without You • Could I Have This Dance? • Endless Love • I. O. U. • Let It Be Me • Love Is Here To Stay • Love Me Tender • Misty • My Cup Runneth Over • My Funny Valentine • September Morn • Share Your Love With Me • She Believes In Me • Sunrise, Sunset • Through The Years • True Love • Try To Remember • You Needed Me • Your Song.

206. FAVORITE CHILDREN'S SONGS $6.95   00101585
33 children's favorites, including: Chim Chim Cher-ee • Happy Birthday To You • I Whistle A Happy Tune • It's A Small World • Old MacDonald Had A Farm • Peter Cottontail • The Rainbow Connection • and more.

207. JIM HENSON'S MUPPETS™ $5.95   00101698
18 favorites, including: Mah-na, Mah-na • The Muppet Show Theme • The Rainbow Connection.

208. CHRISTMAS WITH THE MUPPETS™ $6.95   00101553
21 holiday songs including: Away In A Manger • I Heard The Bells On Christmas Day • O Come All Ye Faithful • O Little Town Of Bethlehem • Silent Night.

209. DISNEY CHRISTMAS FAVORITES $5.95   00101570
24 holiday favorites, including: Deck The Hall • Hark! The Herald Angels Sing • Jingle Bells • O Come All Ye Faithful • Silent Night • and more.

211. THE BEST OF MADONNA $5.95   00101778
10 of this 80's superstar's best, including: Angel • Borderline • Dress You Up • Holiday • Like A Virgin • Live To Tell • Lucky Star • Material Girl • Papa Don't Preach • True Blue.

212. CHART HITS OF THE 80'S $8.95   00101552
27 songs, including: Everytime You Go Away • I. O. U. • Neutron Dance • Sara • There'll Be Sad Songs (To Make You Cry) • These Dreams • You Give Good Love • Will You Still Love Me?

213. BIG BOOK OF DISNEY SONGS $16.95   00101546
42 of Disney's best, including: The Bare Necessities • Chim Chim Cher-ee • It's A Small World • Mickey Mouse March • Some Day My Prince Will Come • Winnie The Pooh • Zip-A-Dee-Doo-Dah • more!

214. TOP CHART HITS $9.95   00102030
21 songs, including: At This Moment • Glory Of Love • Higher Love • Livin' On A Prayer • Papa Don't Preach • True Blue • Word Up • more.

215. THE BEST CHRISTMAS SONGS EVER $14.95   00101533
76 favorite holiday tunes, including: Away In A Manger • The First Noel • Frosty The Snow Man • Jingle Bells • Let It Snow! Let It Snow! Let It Snow! • O Come All Ye Faithful • Rudolph The Red-Nosed Reindeer • Silent Night • The Twelve Days Of Christmas • more.

216. RICHARD CLAYDERMAN —HOLLYWOOD & BROADWAY $7.95   00101556
12 songs recorded by this world renowned pianist. Includes: All The Things You Are • If I Loved You • Night And Day • People.

217. 25 TOP TV HITS $6.95   00102042
25 popular melodies from television, including: Dallas • The Theme From The Greatest American Hero • Hawaii Five-O • Miami Vice • Mickey Mouse March • Secret Agent Man • more.

218. MORE GOSPEL SONGS OF BILL & GLORIA GAITHER $10.95   00101617
50 songs of love and worship written by this well-known Christian couple.

219. CHART TOPPERS $8.95   00101554
22 recent hits, including: Be Still My Beating Heart • Candle In The Wind • Could've Been • Faith • Got My Mind Set On You • Man In The Mirror • With Or Without You.

220. WEDDING SONGS OF LOVE & FRIENDSHIP $7.95   00102072
28 songs of devotion, including: Doubly Good To You • Because • I Am Loved • Longer • The Lord's Prayer • Portrait Of Love • Sunrise, Sunset • What A Difference You've Made In My Life.

221. THE RANDY TRAVIS SONGBOOK $9.95   00102035
20 of his greatest hits, including: Diggin' Up Bones • Forever And Ever, Amen • On The Other Hand.

222. CONTEMPORARY COUNTRY $6.95   00101557
24 hit country tunes, including: Always Late With Your Kisses • Daddy's Hands • Famous Last Words Of A Fool • Forever And Ever, Amen • I'll Still Be Loving You • Love Will Find Its Way To You • Ocean Front Property • Straight To The Heart • Turn It Loose.

223. GLORIOUS PRAISE $6.95   00101614
26 songs of worship and praise, including: Find A Way • Friends • How Excellent Is Thy Name • How Majestic Is Your Name • Via Dolorosa.

224. AMY GRANT GREATEST HITS $7.95   00101458
21 of this Christian superstar's best songs, including: Find A Way • Tennessee Christmas • Angels • El Shaddai • Doubly Good To You.

225. THE LAWRENCE WELK SONGBOOK $9.95   00102080
51 great songs made famous by Lawrence Welk, including: Apples And Bananas • Bubbles In The Wine • Calcutta • Mack The Knife • The Poor People Of Paris • The Wayward Wind.

226. THE AWARD-WINNING SONGS OF THE COUNTRY MUSIC ASSOCIATION $15.95   00101482
More than 70 terrific country songs, including: Always On My Mind • Before The Next Teardrop Falls • Daddy Sang Bass • D-I-V-O-R-C-E • Elvira • The Gambler • Ode To Billy Joe • Southern Nights • Take This Job And Shove It.

227. MICHAEL W. SMITH GREATEST HITS $7.95   00101943
25 great tunes from this very popular Christian singer/songwriter. Includes: Angels • Find A Way • Friends • How Majestic Is Your Name • Thy Word • To The Praise Of His Glorious Grace.

228. SONGS OF THE 20'S $12.95   00101931
56 songs, including: Ain't Misbehavin' • Among My Souvenirs • Button up Your Overcoat • Everybody Loves My Baby • Look For The Silver Lining • Yes! We Have No Bananas.

229. SONGS OF THE 30'S $12.95   00101932
58 songs, including: All Of Me • A Foggy Day • My Funny Valentine • Pennies From Heaven • You're My Everything.

230. SONGS OF THE 40'S $12.95   00101933
62 songs, including: Anniversary Song • Come Rain Or Come Shine • How High The Moon • People Will Say We're 'n Love • The Things We Did Last Summer.

231. SONGS OF THE 50'S $12.95   00101934
60 songs, including: All I HaveTo Do Is Dream • Blue Suede Shoes • Crying In The Chapel • Here's That Rainy Day • Shake, Rattle And Roll • Young At Heart.

232. SONGS OF THE 60'S $12.95   00101935
61 songs, including: As Long As He Needs Me • By The Time I Get To Phoenix • The Girl From Ipanema • If I Had A Hammer • Monday, Monday • Please, Please Me.

233. SONGS OF THE 70'S $12.95   00101936
49 songs, including: After The Love Has Gone • Daniel • Feelings • Joy To The World • Let It Be • Mandy • Send In The Clowns.

234. THE BEST OF BILLY OCEAN $6.95   00101822
10 of his best, including: Caribbean Queen • Get Outta My Dreams, Get Into My Car • Suddenly • When The Going Gets Tough, The Tough Get Going.

235. ELVIS PRESLEY ANTHOLOGY $12.95   00101581
59 songs, including: All Shook Up • Are You Lonesome Tonight • Heartbreak Hotel • Hound Dog • In The Ghetto • Love Me Tender • Suspicious Minds.

236. 25 CHART HITS $7.95   00290055
25 chart-toppping hits, including: Every Rose Has Its Thorn • Fast Car • Kokomo • Lost In Your Eyes • One More Try.

237. ROCK REVIVAL $6.95   00290056
29 top hits from the early rock era, including: Chantilly Lace • Don't Be Cruel • Louie Louie • Splish Splash • The Twist • Wooly Booly • and more.

238. 25 TOP CHRISTMAS SONGS $7.95   00290059
25 favorite Christmas tunes, including: Frosty The Snow Man • Home For The Holidays • Jingle Bell Rock • Santa Claus Is Coming To Town.

239. BIG BOOK OF CHILDREN'S SONGS $10.95   00290170
89 songs that children love. Includes: The Animal Fair • Be Kind To Your Web-Footed Friends • Camptown Races • The Crawdad Song • For He's A Jolly Good Fellow • Humpty Dumpty • Hush, Little Baby • John Jacob Jingleheimer Schmitt • Little Brown Jug • The Old Grey Mare • Ring Around The Rosie • Shortnin' Bread • Twinkle, Twinkle Little Star • and more.

240. FRANK SINATRA SONGBOOK $18.95   00290120
92 songs recorded by Sinatra, including: All The Way • The Birth Of The Blues • High Hopes • I've Got You Under My Skin • The Lady Is A Tramp • Love And Marriage • Nancy (With The Laughing Face) • Theme From New York, New York • Night And Day • Summer Wind • Three Coins In The Fountain • Time After Time • Witchcraft • Young At Heart.

241. THE BEST OF DEBBIE GIBSON $6.95   00290206
12 songs by this teen sensation, including: Electric Youth • Foolish Beat • Lost In Your Eyes • No More Rhyme • Only In My Dreams • Out Of The Blue • Shake Your Love • Staying Together.

242. LES MISERABLES $7.95   00290209
13 songs from the musical smash hit. Includes: Castle On A Cloud • I Dreamed A Dream • On My Own.

243. THE BEST OF AIR SUPPLY $6.95   00290216
13 songs from this superstar pop duo. Includes: All Out Of Love • Even The Nights Are Better • Every Woman In The World • Here I Am • Lost In Love • Making Love Out Of Nothing At All • The One That You Love • and more.

244. SONGS OF THE 80'S $12.95   00290242
49 top hits, including: Careless Whisper • Don't Worry Be Happy • Ebony And Ivory • Endless Love • Every Breath You Take • Fast Car • Hard Habit To Break • I Want To Know What Love Is • Islands In The Stream • Kokomo • Lost In Your Eyes • Memory • One More Try • I'll Be Loving You (Forever) • We Didn't Start The Fire • Sailing • Sara • Soldier Of Love • These Dreams • Total Eclipse Of The Heart • What's Love Got To Do With It • With Or Without You.

245. NEW KIDS ON THE BLOCK — HANGIN' TOUGH $6.95   00290237
10 songs from these teen sensations, including: Please Don't Go Girl • I'll Be Loving You (Forever) • Hangin' Tough • (You've Got It) The Right Stuff • Cover Girl.

246. A TREASURY OF SONGS $17.95   00102081
A huge collection of 78 contemporary favorites, including: American Pie • The Birds And The Bees • Do You Know The Way To San Jose • Eye In The Sky • Imagine • Longer • Lost In Love • Piano Man • Raindrops Keep Fallin' On My Head • Sailing • Walk On By • You're Having My Baby • much more.

247. TOP COUNTRY FAVORITES $6.95   00290264
24 country hits, including: Above And Beyond • All The Gold In California • Come On In • Forever And Ever Amen • From Graceland To The Promised Land • God Bless The U.S.A. • Lookin' For Love • You Decorated My Life.

248. LITTLE MERMAID $8.95   00102108
The matching folio to this Disney hit movie, including the Oscar-winning "Under The Sea" and 7 others: Daughters Of Triton • Fathoms Below • Kiss The Girl • more.

249. CHART PICKS $7.95   00102109
18 big chart hits, including: How Am I Supposed To Live Without You • All Around The World • Hold On • Black Velvet • We Didn't Start The Fire • and more.

250. TEENAGE MUTANT NINJA TURTLES $8.95   00102110
8 radical turtle tunes from the movie sensation, including: Spin That Wheel • T-U-R-T-L-E Power! • Every Heart Needs A Home • Turtle Rhapsody. Also includes many color photos from the movie itself.
TEENAGE MUTANT NINJA TURTLES is a registered trademark of Mirage Studios U.S.A. Exclusively licensed by Surge Licensing.

251. THE PHANTOM OF THE OPERA $7.95   00102113
9 songs from this Broadway smash, including: All I Ask Of You • The Point Of No Return • The Phantom Of The Opera • and more.

252. GLORIA ESTEFAN AND MIAMI SOUND MACHINE GREATEST HITS $7.95   00102138
14 of their best including, Bad Boy • 1-2-3 • Rhythm Is Gonna Get You • Words Get In The Way • Don't Wanna Lose You and many more.

253. HOT POPS $9.95   00102119
25 current chartbusters from today's biggest stars, including: Another Day In Paradise • The End Of The Innocence • Escapade • If I Could Turn Back Time • The Living Years • Nothing Compares 2U • Vogue • and more!

255. BILLBOARD SERIES—BEST OF 1955 $6.95   00290189
15 songs from 1955, including: Rock Around The Clock • Sixteen Tons • Autumn Leaves • Dance With Me Henry • Hearts Of Stone • Earth Angel • Moments To Remember • Only You (And You Alone).

256. BILLBOARD SERIES—BEST OF 1956 $6.95   00290190
15 songs from 1956, including: Don't Be Cruel • Hound Dog • The Wayward Wind • My Prayer • The Green Door • Que Sera, Sera • True Love • No, Not Much.

257. BILLBOARD SERIES—BEST OF 1957 $6.95   00290191
15 songs from 1957, including: All Shook Up • Jailhouse Rock • Wake Up, Little Susie • Chances Are • Party Doll • Blueberry Hill • Peggy Sue • Tammy.

258. BILLBOARD SERIES—BEST OF 1958 $6.95   00290192
15 songs from 1958, including: At The Hop • Purple People Eater • All I Have To Do Is Dream • It's Only Make Believe • Get A Job • Tom Dooley • Great Balls Of Fire • Lollipop.

259. BILLBOARD SERIES—BEST OF 1959 $6.95   00290193
15 songs from 1959, including: Mack The Knife • Battle Of New Orleans • Venus • Sleep Walk • Kansas City • Personality • Sixteen Candles • Charlie Brown.

260. BILLBOARD SERIES—BEST OF 1960 $6.95   00102142
15 songs from 1960, including: The Theme From "A Summer Place" • It's Now Or Never • I'm Sorry • Running Bear • Save The Last Dance For Me • The Twist • Alley Oop • Stay.

261. BILLBOARD SERIES—BEST OF 1961 $6.95   00102115
15 songs, including: Runaway • Pony Time • The Lion Sleeps Tonight • Runaround Sue • Will You Love Me Tomorrow • Hit The Road Jack • Moody River.

262. BILLBOARD SERIES—BEST OF 1962 $6.95   00102116
15 songs including: Big Girls Don't Cry • Sherry • Duke Of Earl • Breaking Up Is Hard To Do • The Loco-Motion • Return To Sender • The Stripper.

263. BILLBOARD SERIES—BEST OF 1963 $6.95   00102117
15 hits including: Dominique • My Boyfriend's Back • Blue Velvet • I Will Follow Him • Walk Like A Man • Surf City • It's My Party • Louie, Louie

264. BILLBOARD SERIES—BEST OF 1964 $6.95   00102118
15 songs including: Chapel Of Love • I Want To Hold Your Hand • She Loves You • Hello, Dolly! • Rag Doll • Leader Of The Pack.

290. NEWS KIDS ON THE BLOCK— STEP BY STEP $7.95   00102120
12 songs from the latest release of this superstar group. Feautres: Step By Step • Tonight • Games • Happy Birthday • and more.

293. MOVIE CLASSICS $8.95   00102124
37 of the best songs from silver screen classics, including: A Time For Us • Chitty Chitty Bang Bang • Live And Let Die • Love Is A Many Splendored Thing • Moon River • Over The Rainbow • The Pink Panther • Singin' In The Rain • Talk To The Animals • Theme From New York, New York • You Light Up My Life.

294. 54 STANDARD HITS $10.95   00102127
54 favorites, including: Blue Hawaii • Don't It Make My Brown Eyes Blue • Georgia On My Mind • Love Makes The World Go Round • Moon River • Pennsylvania 6-5000 • Roses Are Red My Love • Theme From New York, New York • We've Only Just Begun • and more.

295. 55 STANDARD HITS $10.95   00102128
55 more favorites, including: Chattanooga Choo Choo • Games That Lovers Play • Love Letters • San Francisco • Tender Is The Night • Volare • and more.

296. 56 STANDARD HITS $10.95   00102129
56 favorite hits, including: Blue Moon • Hey Look Me Over • I'm Getting Sentimental Over You • Isn't It Romantic • It Don't Mean A Thing (If It Ain't Got That Swing) • Mona Lisa • Singin' In The Rain • That's Amore • The Trolly Song • and more.

297. BEST T.V. THEMES $6.95   00102126
21 of everyone's favorite TV tunes, including: Entertainment Tonight • Jeopardy Theme • The Masterpiece Theater • Thank You For Being A Friend (The Golden Girls) • Theme from "Cheers" • and more.

298. BEAUTIFUL LOVE SONGS $7.95   00102130
27 sentimental favorites, featuring: For Once In My Life • The Greatest Gift Of All • I Honestly Love You • I Just Called To Say I Love You • Love Story • Up Where We Belong • You Are So Beautiful • You Light Up My Life.

299. 19 OF THE 80'S GREATEST HITS $6.95   00102131
20 of the decade's best, including Almost Paradise • Back In The High Life Again • Dancing In The Dark • Glory Of Love • Up Where We Belong.

300. 18 MORE OF THE 80'S GREATEST HITS $6.95   00102132
18 more of the decade's best, including: Against All Odds, Fame • The Greatest Love Of All • (I've Had) The Time Of My Life • Love Shack • On the Wings Of Love • Straight Up • Walk Like An Egyptian.

350. THE BILLBOARD SONGBOOK SERIES— THE BEST OF 1955-1959 $29.95   00102140
This compilation features five books under one cover—80 songs in all with extensive notes on the era and its hits. Song highlights include: Autumn Leaves • Earth Angel • Unchained Melody • Blue Suede Shoes • Hound Dog • All Shook Up • Blueberry Hill • Peggy Sue • At The Hop • The Chipmunk Song • Get A Job • Great Balls Of Fire • Yakety Yak • Donna • Sixteen Candles • Smoke Gets In Your Eyes• and more.

CHRISTMAS LIBRARY $19.80   00100627
A treasury of Christmas magic in this special bound collection of 4 E-Z Play Today songbooks, including: Christmas Songs • That Christmas Feeling • Holly Season • Christmas Time.

COMPLETE ALPHABETICAL SONGFINDER AVAILABLE!
Complete listing of the over 3,000 songs included in the E-Z Play TODAY Songbook Series. Song titles are cross-referenced to the books in which they can be found. Song list also features all titles from the SOLO TODAY, ORGAN ADVENTURE, EASY ELECTRONIC KEYBOARD MUSIC and PORTABLE KEYBOARD MUSIC SERIES.

Available free of charge from your local music store. Or write to: Hal Leonard Publishing Corporation, P.O. Box 13819, Milwaukee, WI 53213. Ask for "Keyboard Alphabetical Songfinder #90500067."

For more infomation, see your local music dealer or write directly to:

Hal Leonard Publishing Corporation
7777 West Bluemound Road P.O. Box 13819 Milwaukee, WI 53213

90600000   4/91

Prices and availability may vary outside the U.S.A. Book prices, contents and availability subject to change.

Lamb Of Glory

Registration 5
Rhythm: Waltz

Words and Music by
Phill McHugh and Greg Nelson

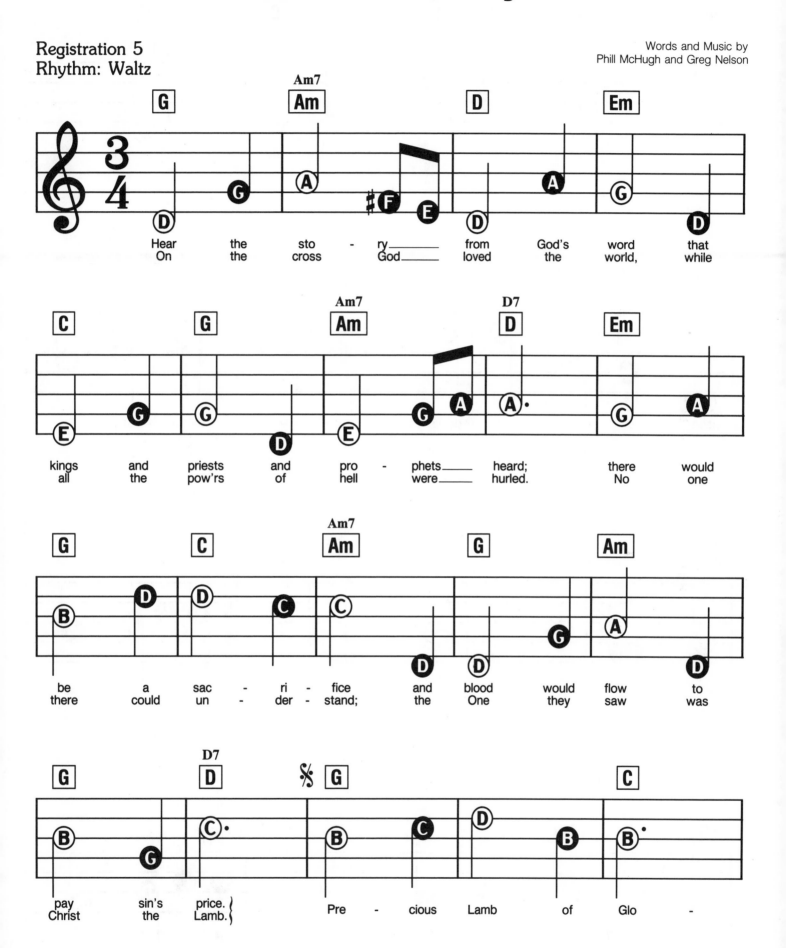

34

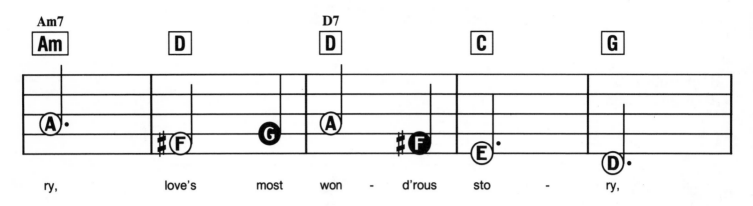

ry,　love's　most　won - d'rous　sto - ry,

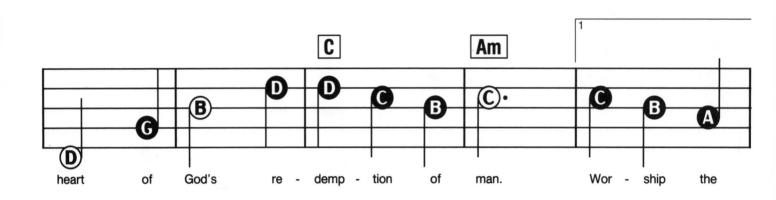

heart　of　God's　re - demp - tion　of　man.　Wor - ship　the

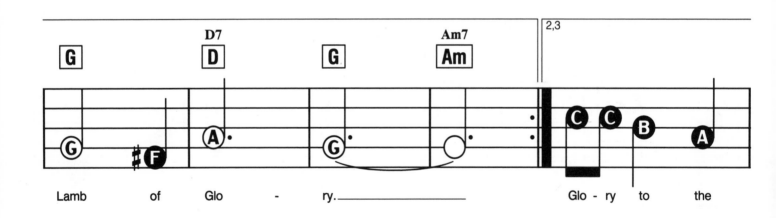

Lamb　of　Glo - ry.　Glo - ry　to　the

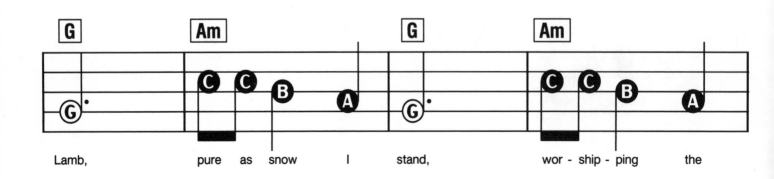

Lamb,　pure　as　snow　I　stand,　wor - ship - ping　the

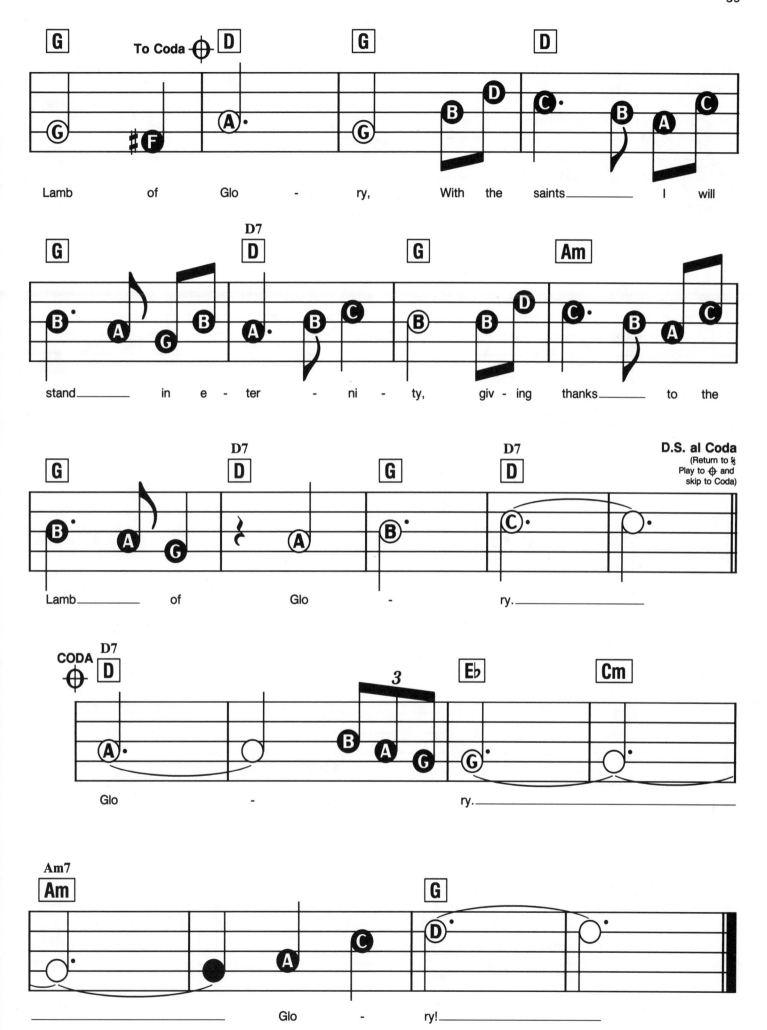

I've A Home Beyond The River

Registration 3
Rhythm: Fox Trot or Swing

By John W. Peterson

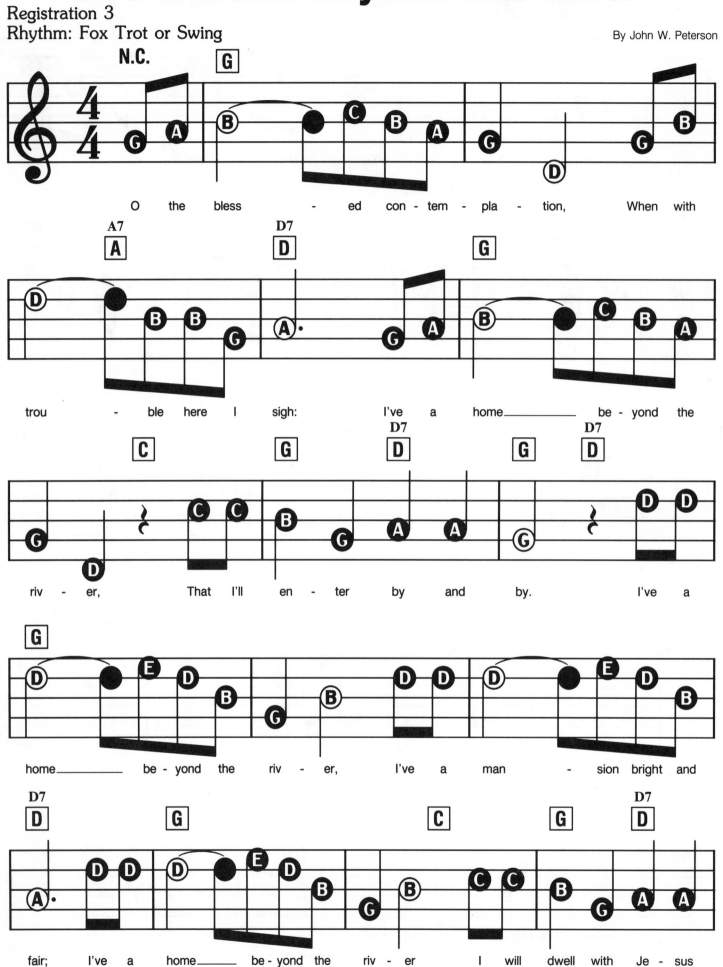

37

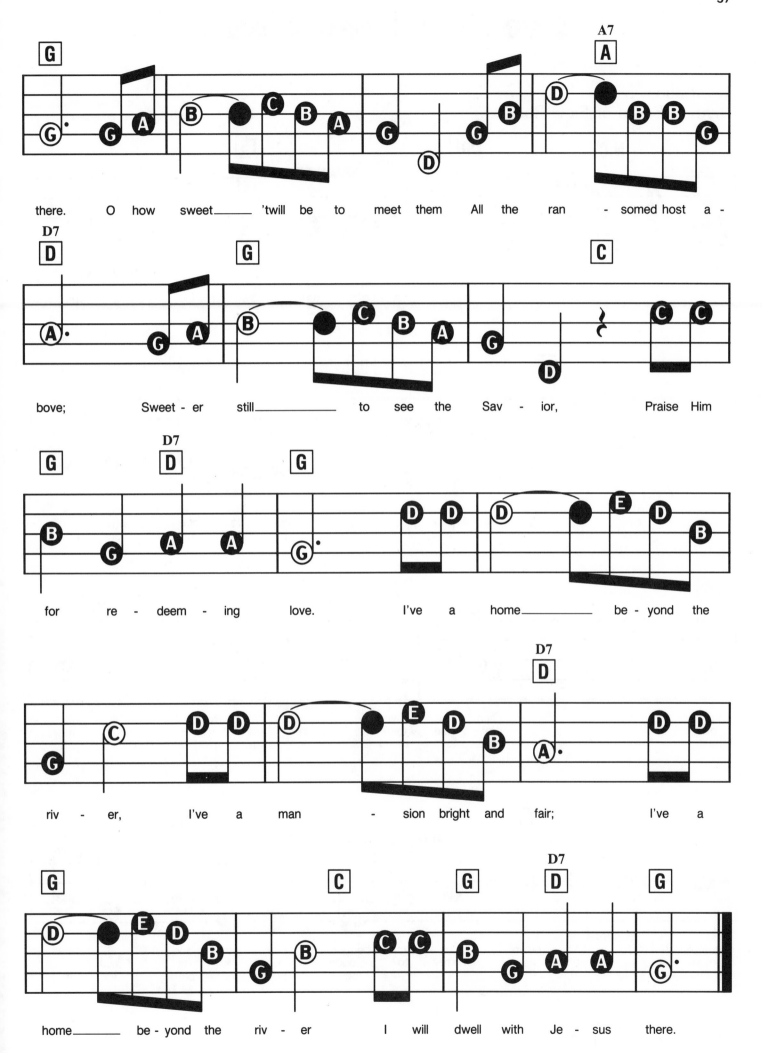

I've Just Seen Jesus

Registration: 3
Rhythm: Ballad or Slow Rock

Words by Gloria Gaither
Music by William J. Gaither and Danny Daniels

39

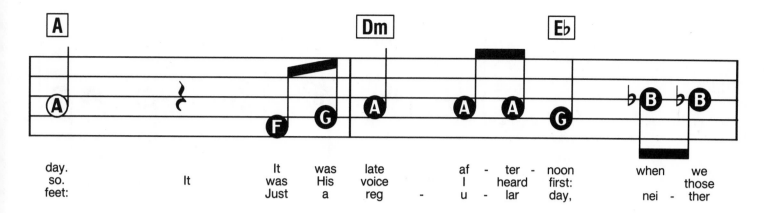

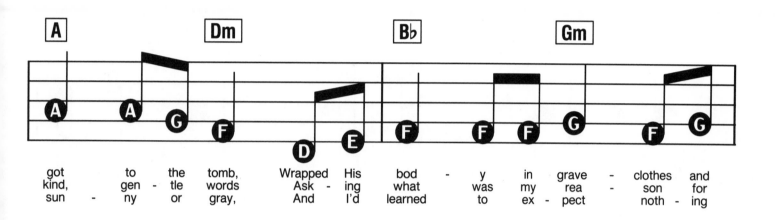

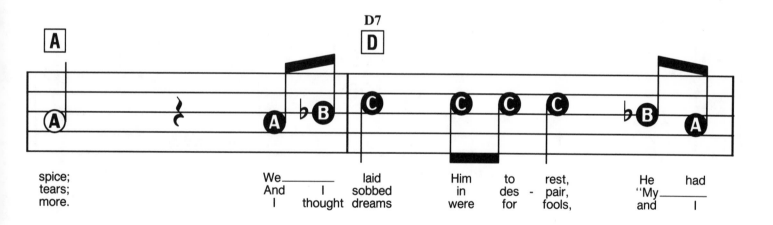

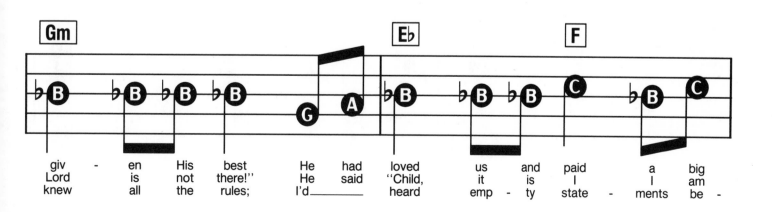

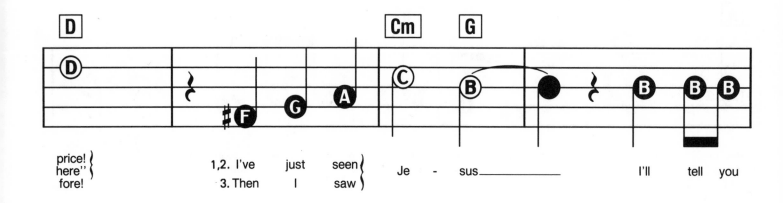

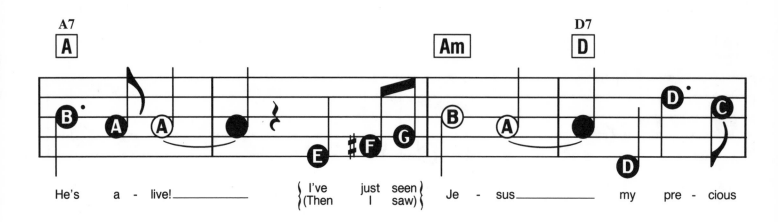

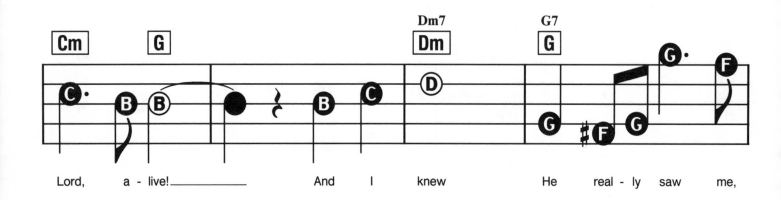

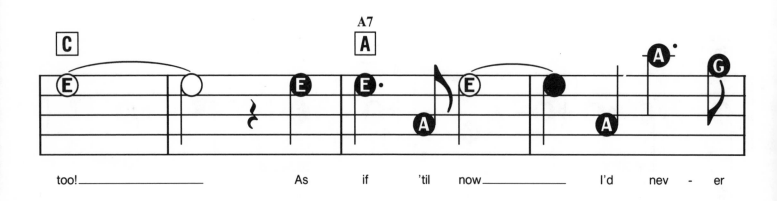

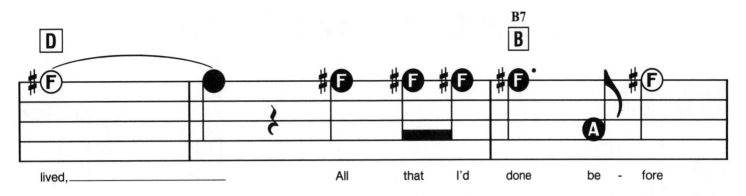

lived,_____ All that I'd done be - fore

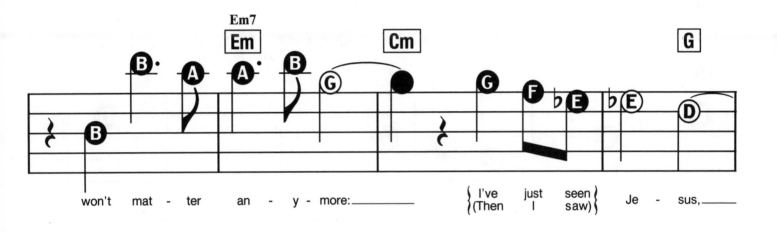

won't mat - ter an - y - more:_____ { I've just seen } Je - sus,_____
{ (Then I saw) }

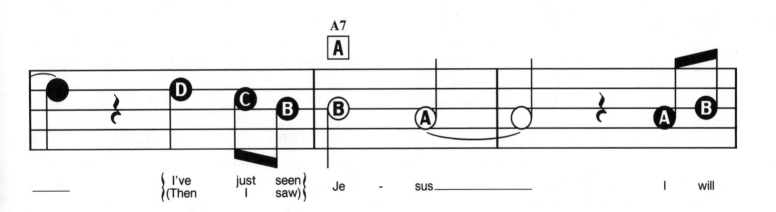

_____ { I've just seen } Je - sus_____ I will
{ (Then I saw) }

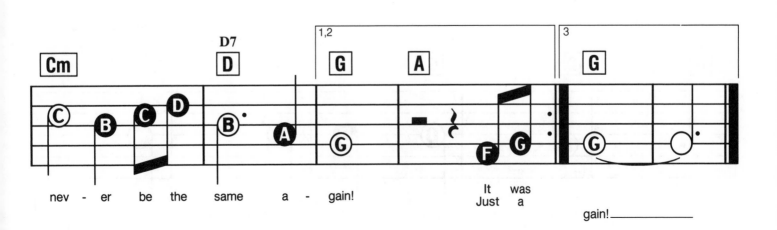

nev - er be the same a - gain! It was
Just a

gain!_____

Jesus Is Coming Again

Registration 1
Rhythm: Waltz

By John W. Peterson

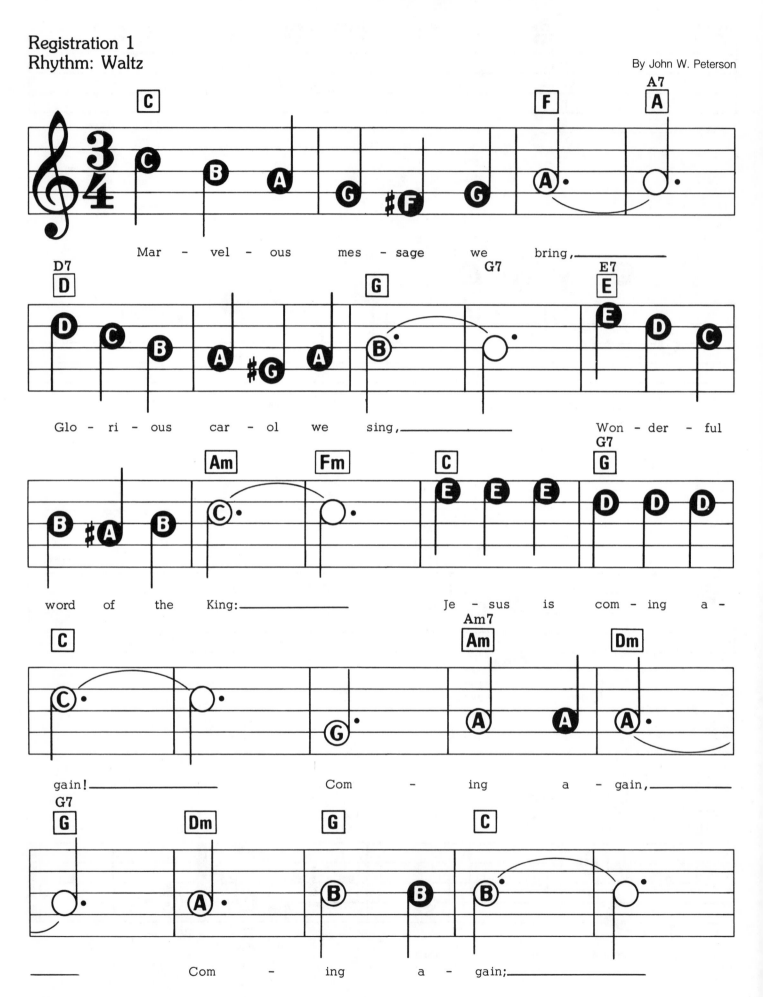

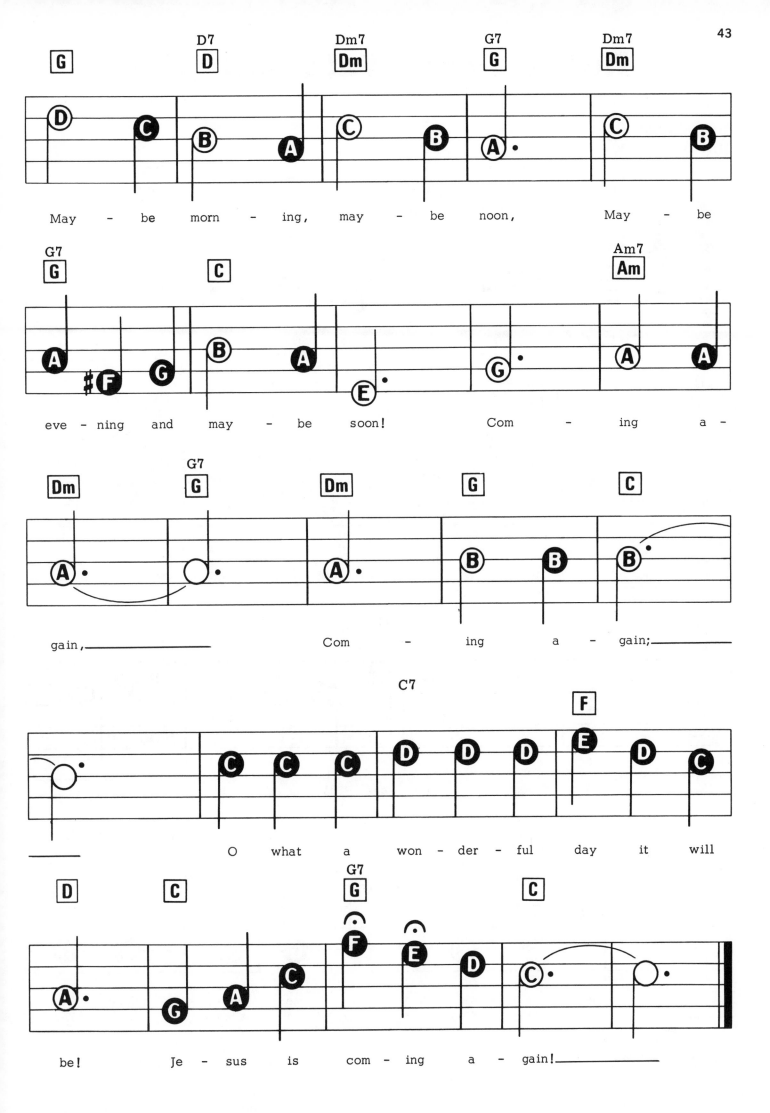

Just A Closer Walk With Thee

Registration 2
Rhythm: Swing

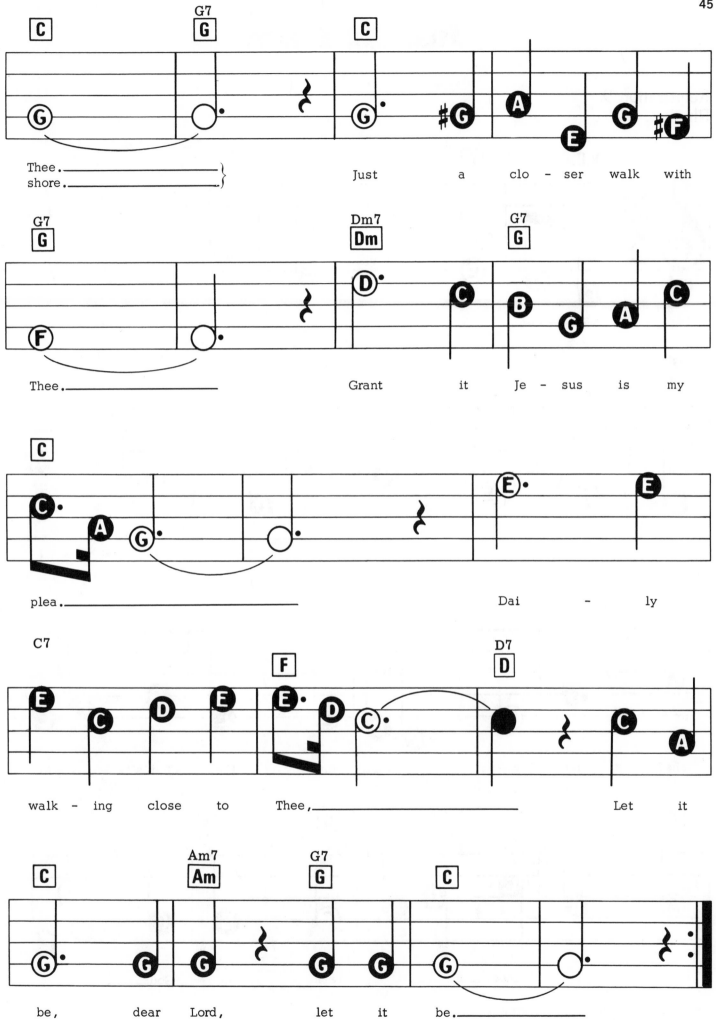

Just As I Am

Registration 9
Rhythm: Waltz

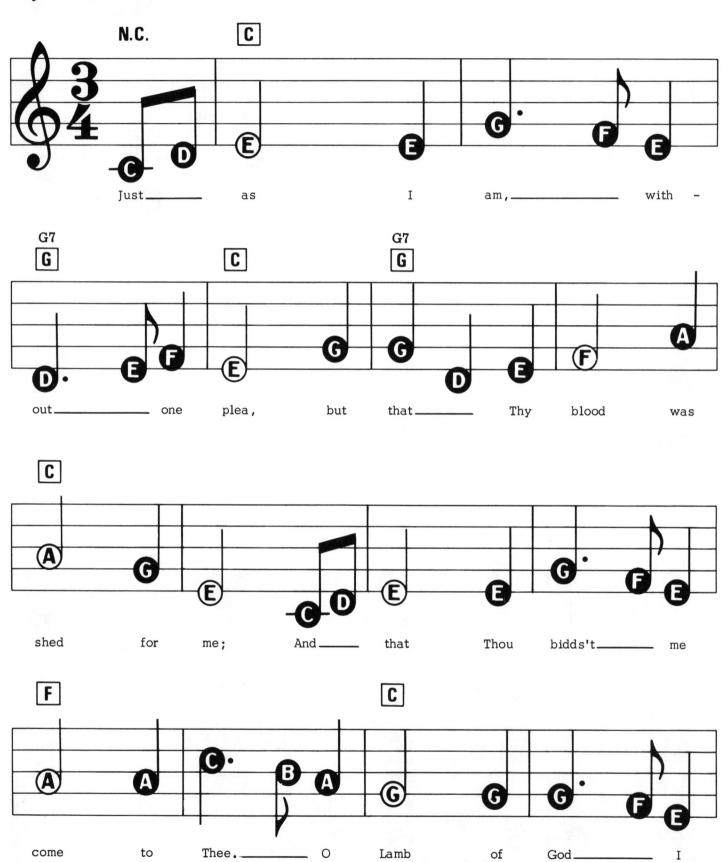

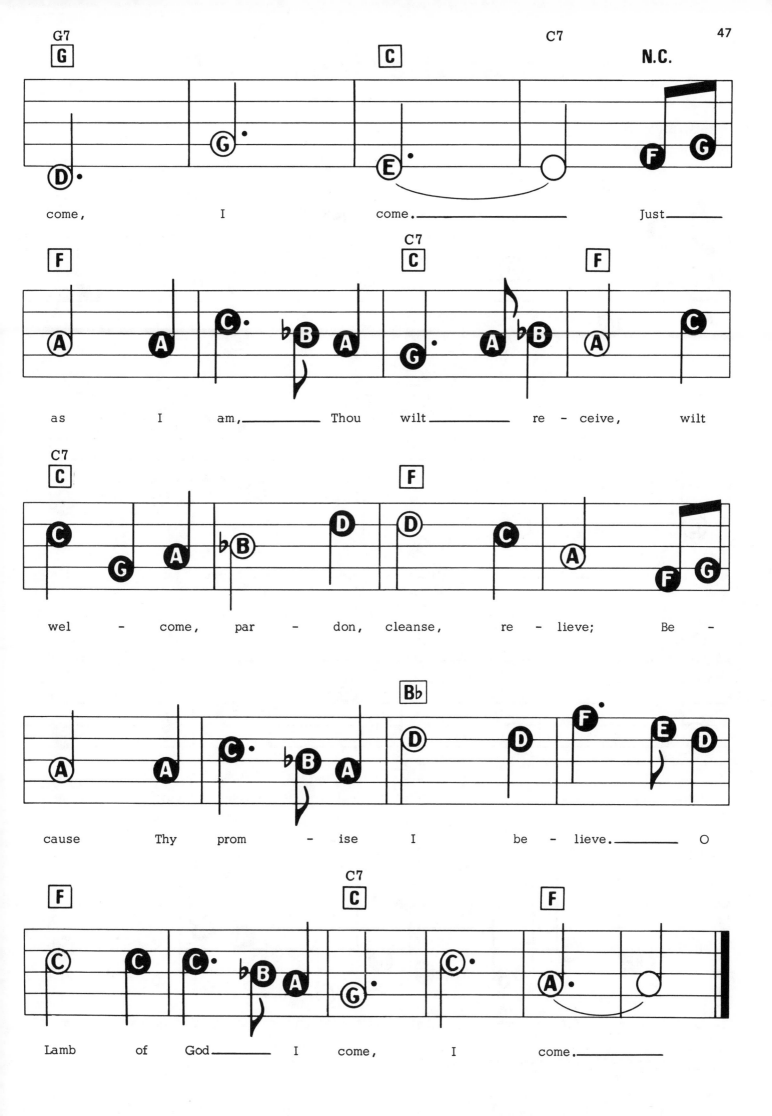

Room At The Cross For You

Registration 5
Rhythm: Waltz

By Ira Stanphill

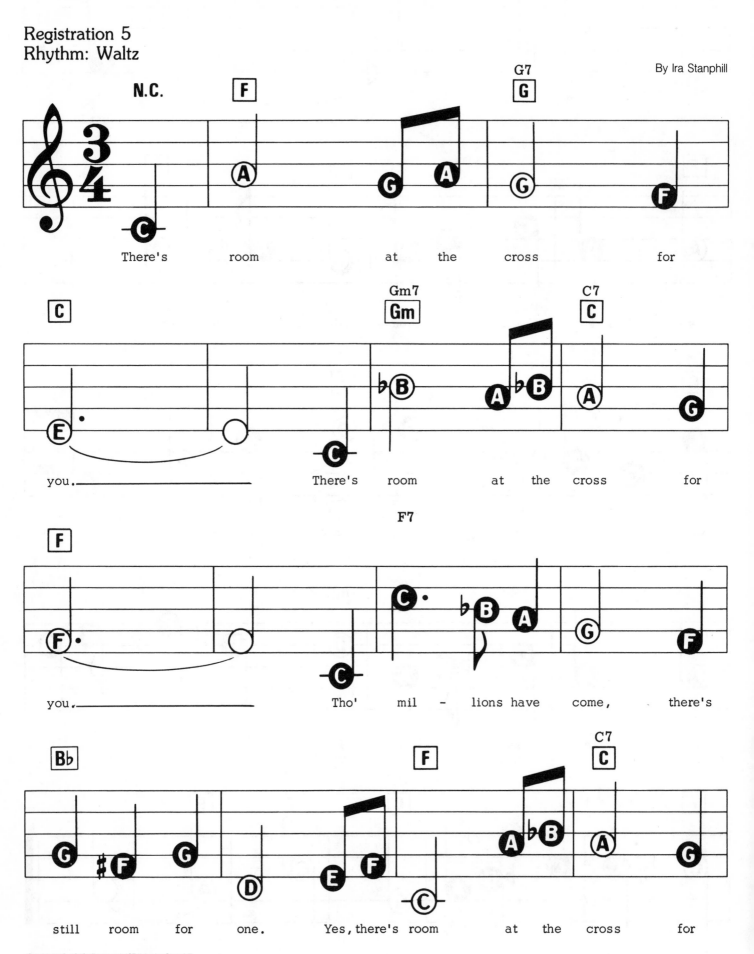

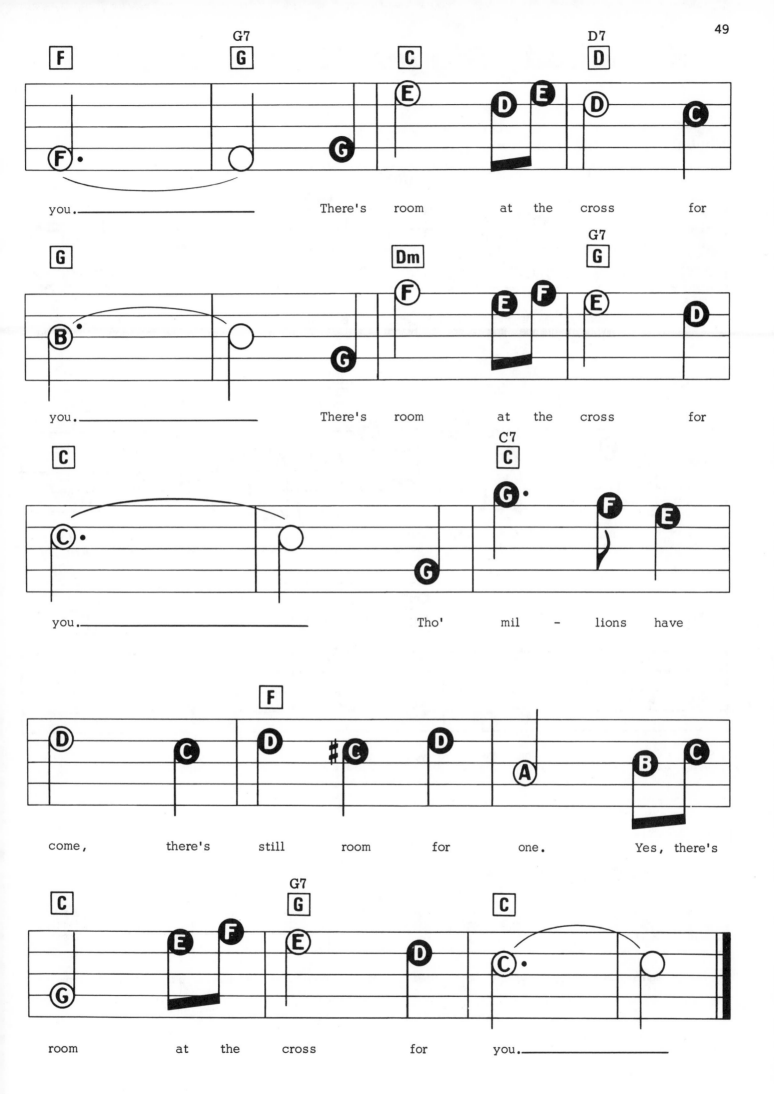

Somebody Bigger Than You And I

Registration 3
Rhythm: Rock or 8 Beat

By Johnny Lange,
Hy Heath and Sonny Burke

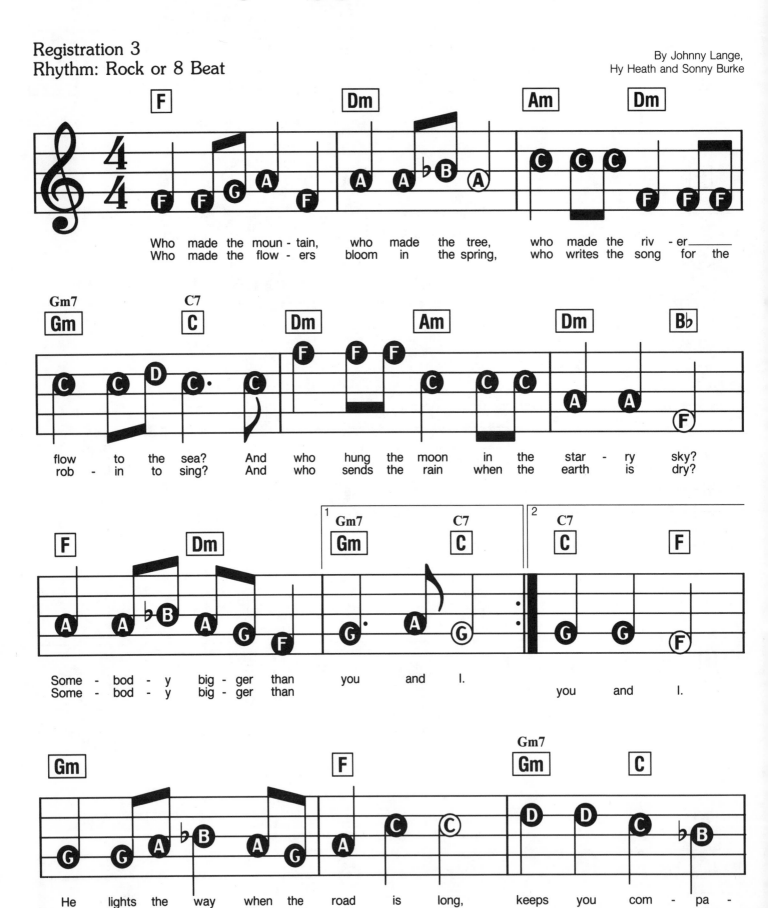

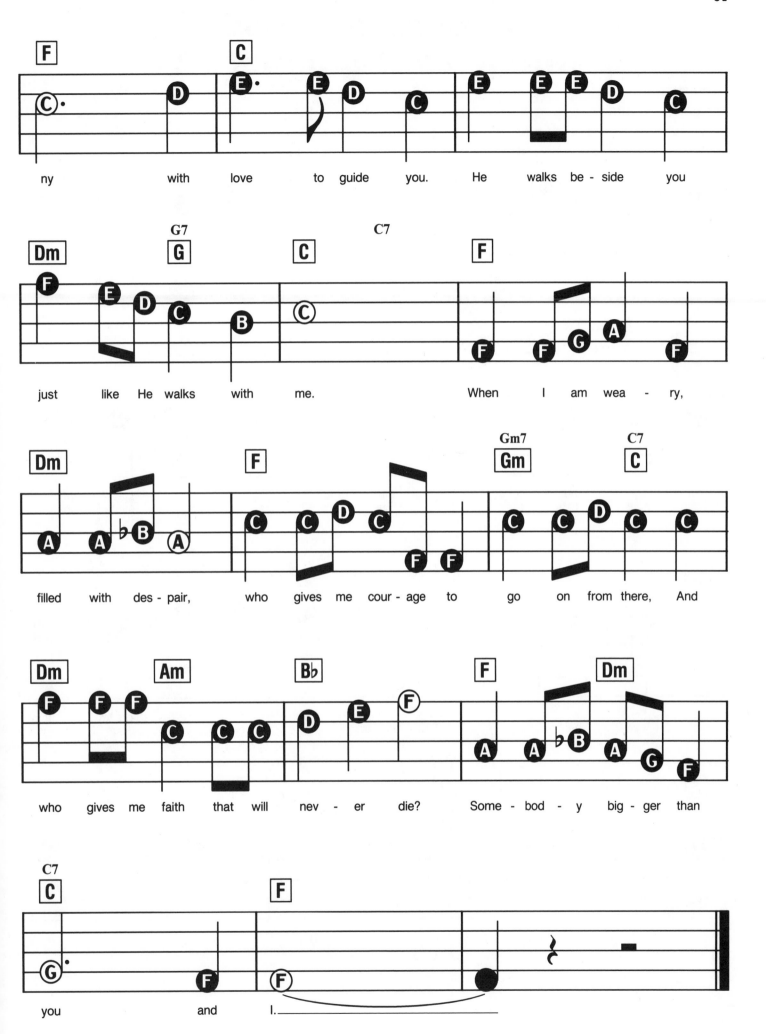

Something Good
Is Going To Happen To You

Registration 10
Rhythm: Waltz

By Ralph Carmichael

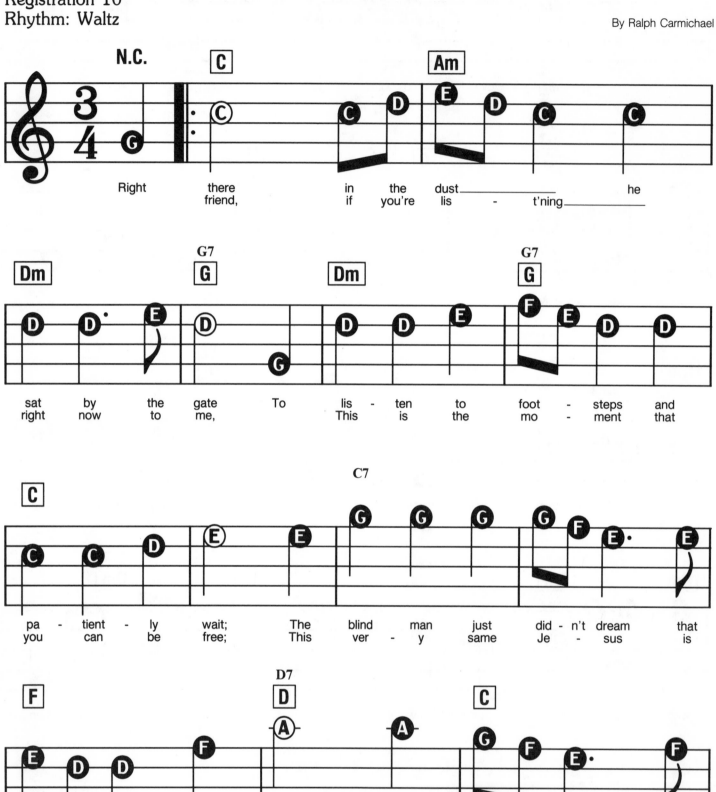

53

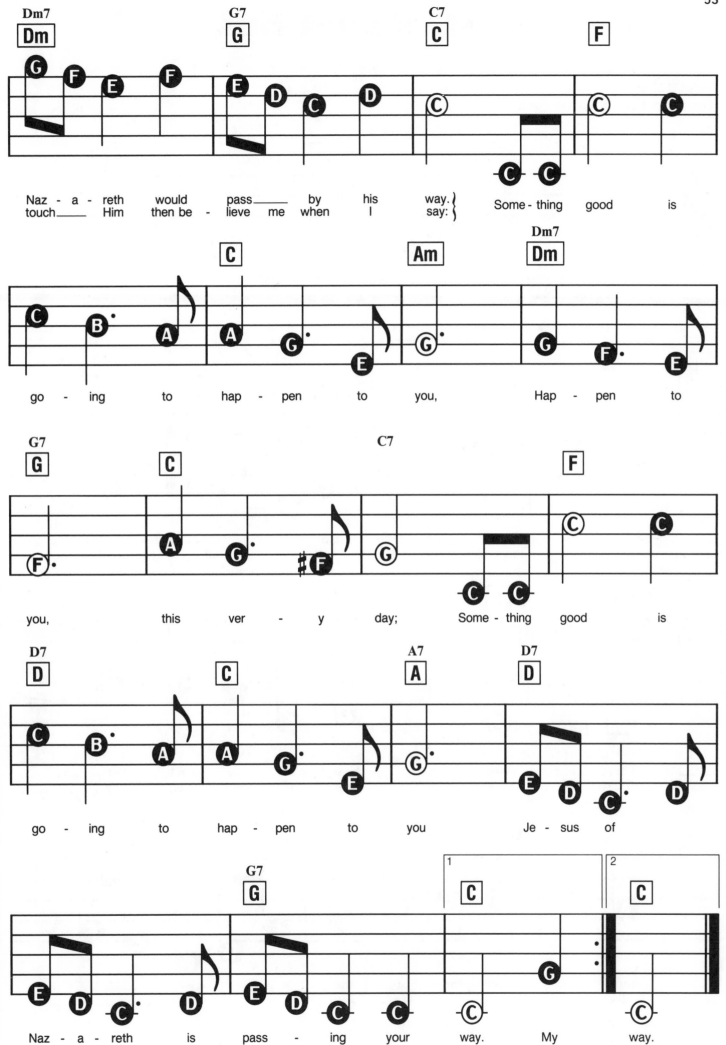

Sweet, Sweet Spirit

Registration 4
Rhythm: Fox Trot or Swing

By Doris Akers

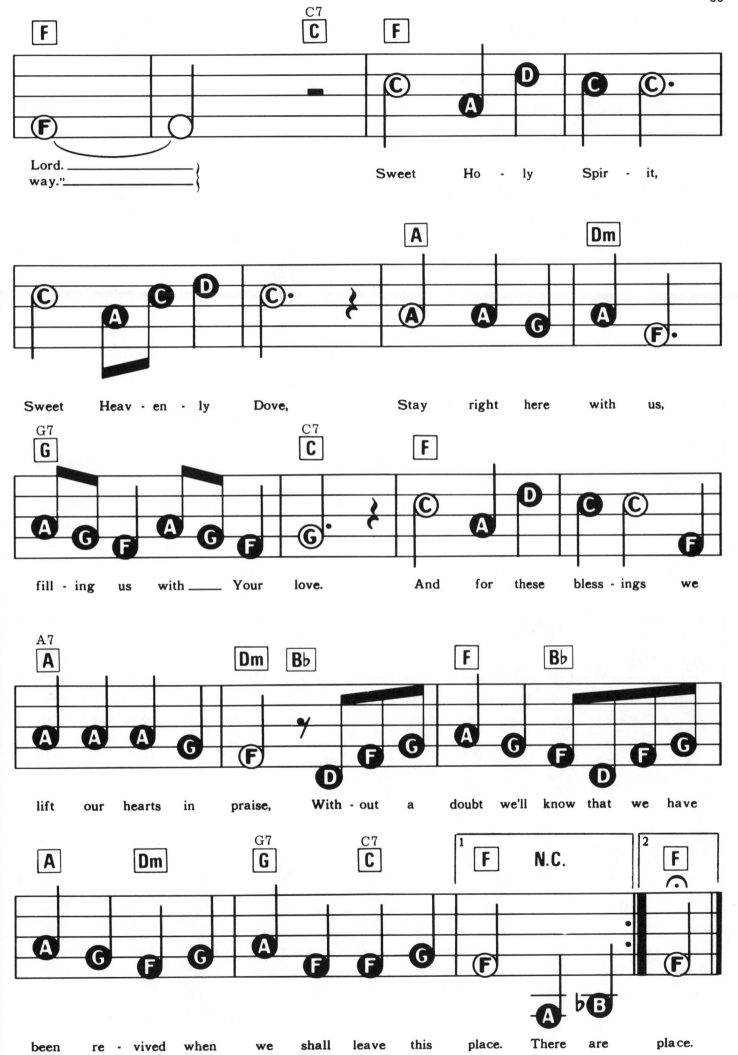

There Is Someone To Help You

Registration 2
Rhythm: Rock or 8 Beat

Words and Music by
Johnny Lange

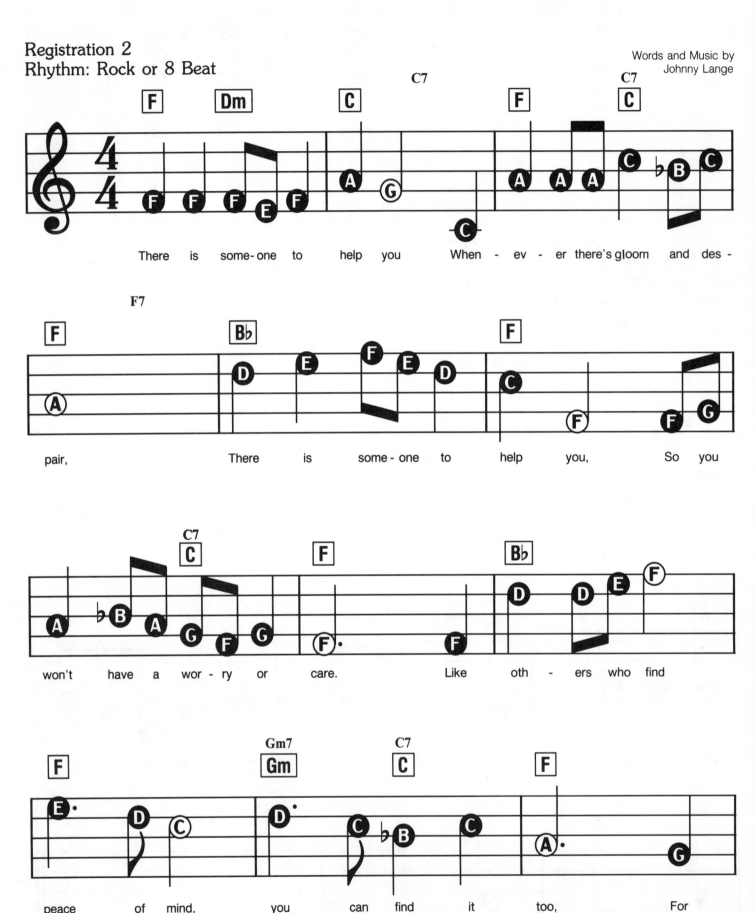

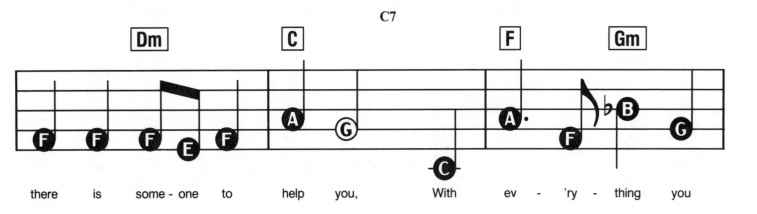

there is some-one to help you, With ev - 'ry - thing you

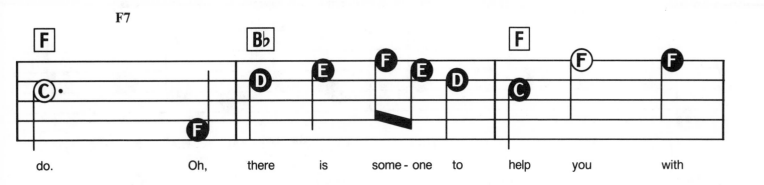

do. Oh, there is some-one to help you with

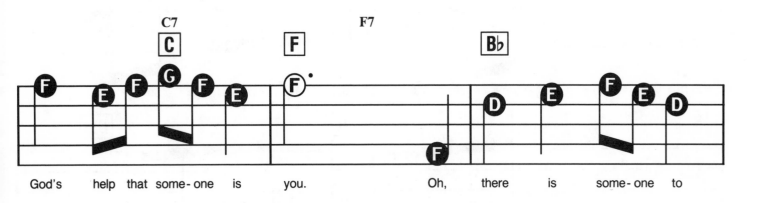

God's help that some-one is you. Oh, there is some-one to

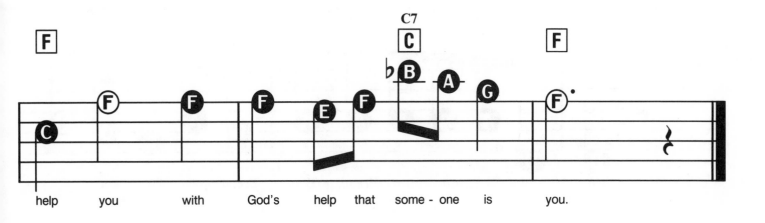

help you with God's help that some-one is you.

To You I Give The Power

Registration 6
Rhythm: Rock or 8 Beat

By Andrew Culverwell

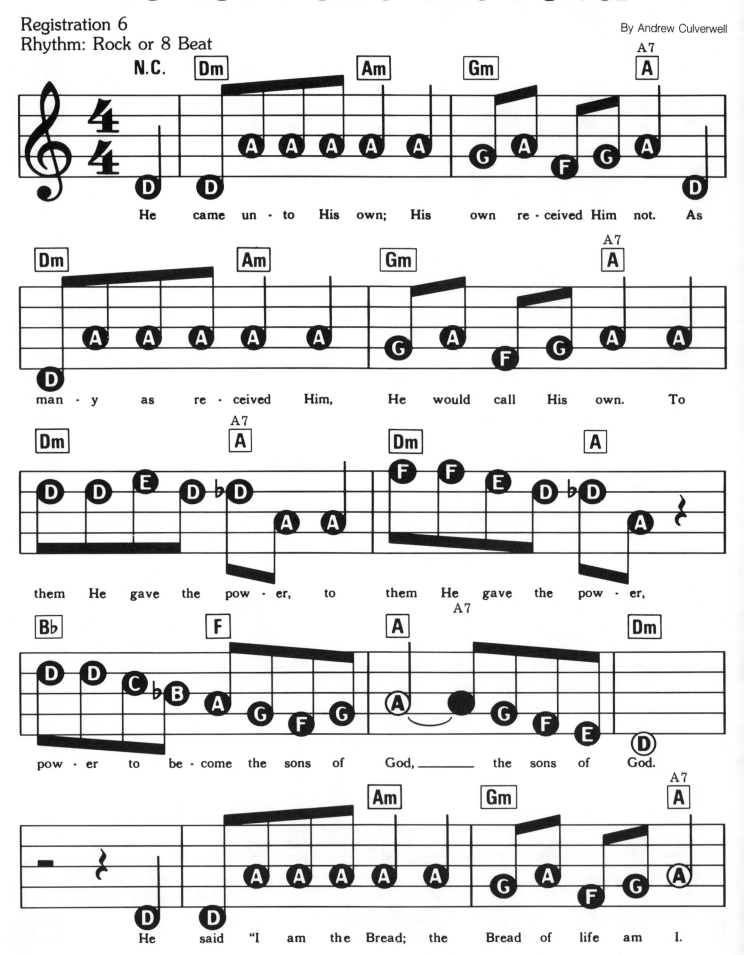

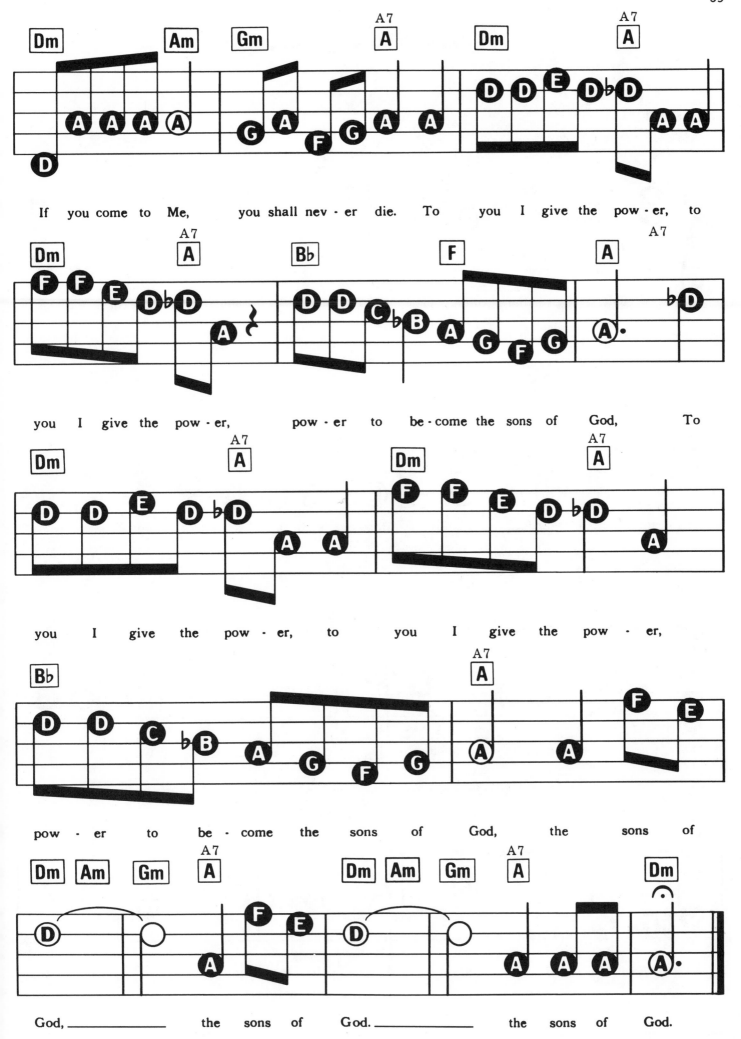

If you come to Me, you shall nev-er die. To you I give the pow-er, to

you I give the pow-er, pow-er to be-come the sons of God, To

you I give the pow-er, to you I give the pow-er,

pow-er to be-come the sons of God, the sons of

God, _____ the sons of God. _____ the sons of God.

Whispering Hope

Registration 10

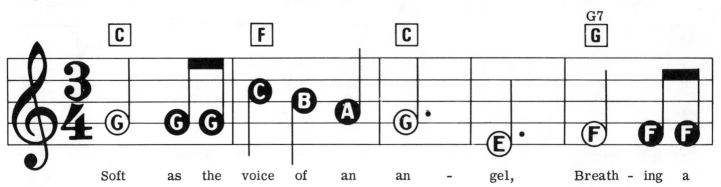

Soft as the voice of an an - gel, Breath - ing a

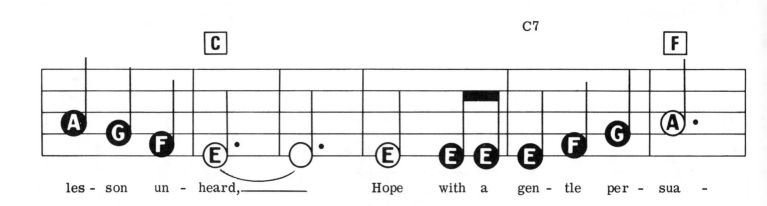

les - son un - heard,_____ Hope with a gen - tle per - sua -

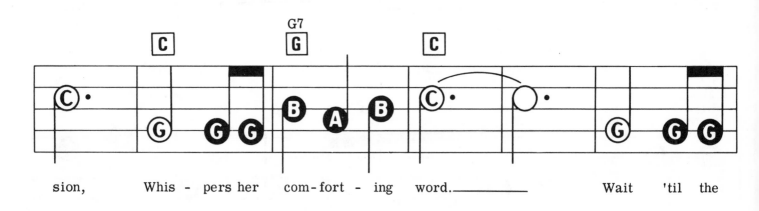

sion, Whis - pers her com - fort - ing word._____ Wait 'til the

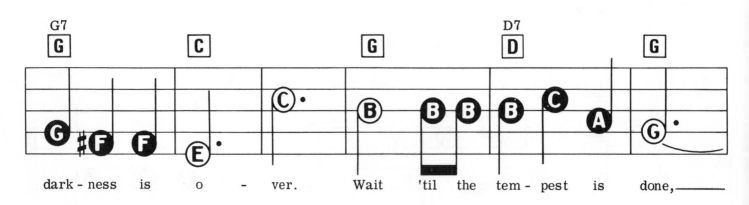

dark - ness is o - ver. Wait 'til the tem - pest is done,_____

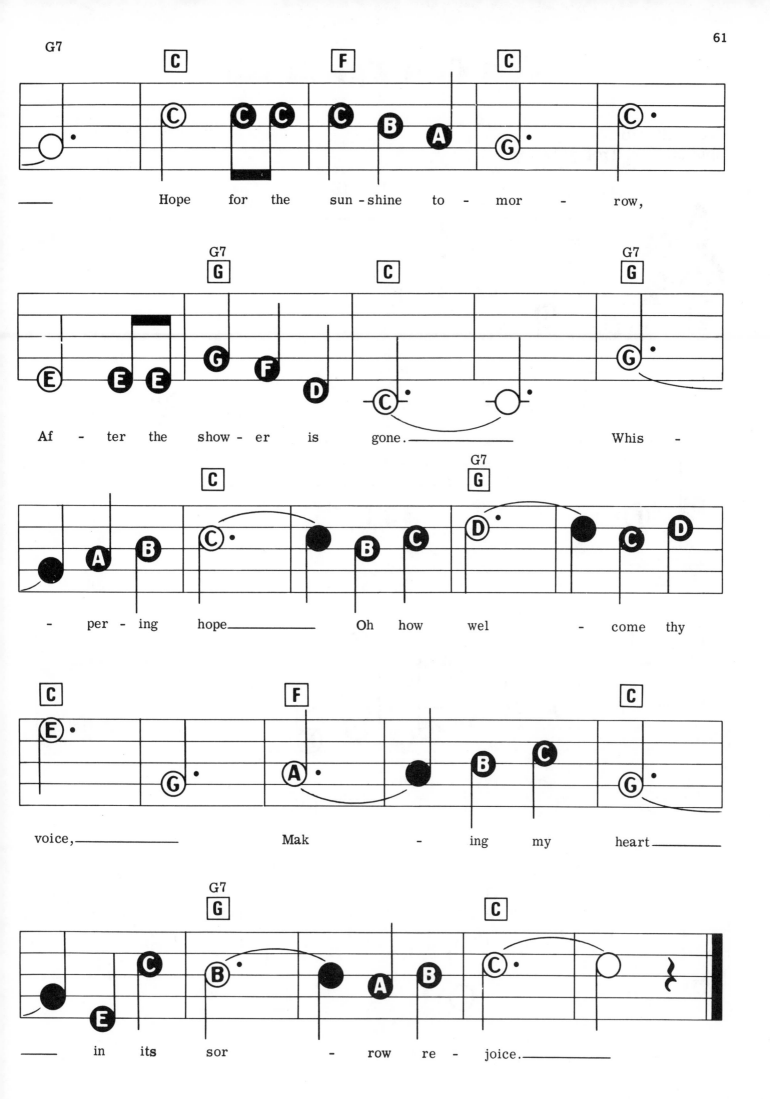

You Can Touch Him

Registration 5
Rhythm: Fox Trot or Swing

By Ralph Carmichael

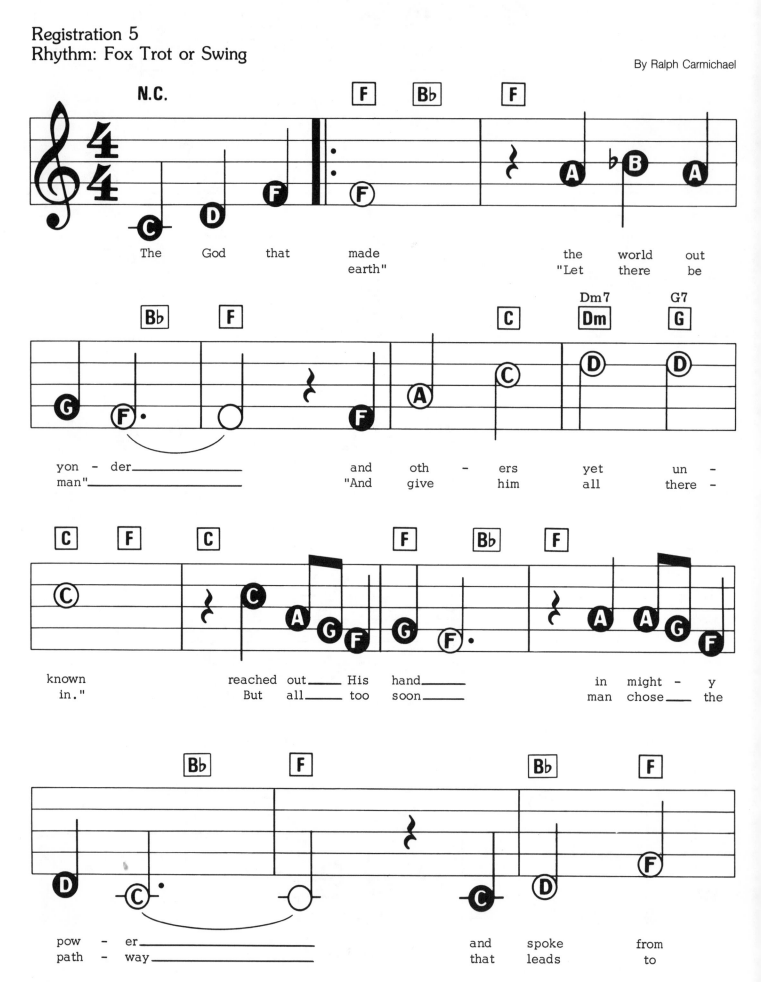

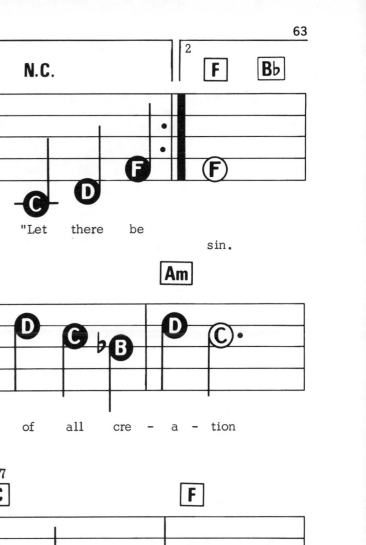

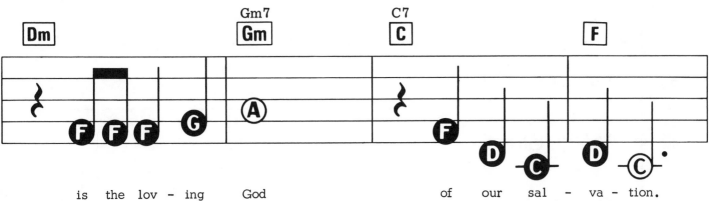

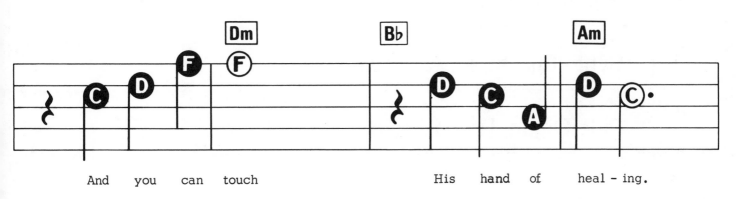

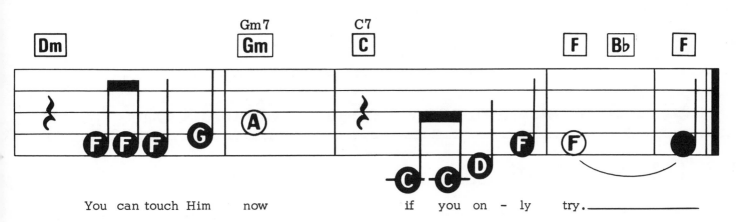

Registration Guide

- Match the Registration number on the song to the corresponding numbered category below. Select and activate an instrumental sound available on your instrument.
- Choose an automatic rhythm appropriate to the mood and style of the song. (Consult your Owner's Guide for proper operation of automatic rhythm features.)
- Adjust the tempo and volume controls to comfortable settings.

Registration

1	Flute, Pan Flute, Jazz Flute
2	Clarinet, Organ
3	Violin, Strings
4	Brass, Trumpet
5	Synth Ensemble, Accordion, Brass
6	Pipe Organ, Harpsichord
7	Jazz Organ, Vibraphone, Vibes, Electric Piano, Jazz Guitar
8	Piano, Electric Piano
9	Trumpet, Trombone, Clarinet, Saxophone, Oboe
10	Violin, Cello, Strings